The InnerGround Railroad

A 40 Day Journey to Remembering Soul & Spirit

QUANITA ROBERSON & **AMY HOWTON**

4515 Allison Street, Suite 12412
Cincinnati, Ohio 45212-9998

Email: info@akanpublishing.com

www.akanpublishing.com

Executive Editor: Quanita Roberson

Illustration & Book Design: Elizabeth H. Murphy
www.illusionstudios.net

Cover: Joseph T. Meirose IV
'Full Frame Works' Photography

Typeset in Constantia & Tratello
ISBN 978-0-578-32041-0
Library of Congress Control Number: 2021922418

First Edition
Copyright 2023 Quanita Roberson
All rights reserved. No part of this book may be reproduced or transmitted in any form or by any means graphic, electronic or mechanical, including photocopying, recording, taping or by any information storage or retrieval system, without the permission in writing from the publisher.
Published by Akan Publishing.

Quanita Roberson & Amy Howton

The InnerGround Railroad

A 40 Day Journey to Remembering Soul & Spirit

This book is dedicated to the ancestors and to the future generations— to those who have come before and to those who are coming after. With *special thanks to Daniel Deardoff, Malidome Somé, Robert Bly, bell hooks, and Archbishop Desmond Tutu*

AKAN PUBLISHING

2023

The InnerGround Railroad

Quanita

I am so grateful to Jacob and Makayla for all the times over these many years that they shared their mother with this book, in the writing and in the times I was growing to be able to write it. Thank you for your patience when I wasn't readily available to you. This book is one of the ways that I mother you. I love you more! And Makayla, yes I do.

Amy, what can I say... I'm glad you said yes. I didn't even know to ask for you but God knew. You have forever changed my life.

Tenneson, thank you for being a friend, colleague and an evolutionary teacher. I am a better person for knowing you.

I also want to thank my elders, Jojopah Maria, Eileen Cooper Reed, Fanchon Shur, Suzanne Stevens, Christina Baldwin and David O'Fallon. I have learned how to listen deeply, open my heart wider, lean into learning, and trust spirit within and without. I hope my work honors you.

And to Beth and Robert for believing from the very beginning that I had something to share worth listening to in the world.

And last but not least to Evalynn, my niece. Who holds the future. Who holds the legacy of who we are to be. I hope our lives honor you. Love you, Auntie Q

Amy

I want to give thanks for my mom, whose choosing herself made room for me. And for my dad, whose choosing us, grew me up. The love you each offered was precisely what was needed. I am so grateful to be your daughter.

For all the teachers and friends and sisters along the way—ya'll know who you are.

For the divinely timed question that Rev. Nelson Pierce offered some time ago that wouldn't let me go: "White people have to know how they have been harmed by White Supremacy...".

For Michael—I am so grateful for you and the life we create together. We have grown each other up and continue to discover the gifts of unconditional love. Somehow, after twenty-five years, you are still my exhale. Thank you for loving me just as you do.

For Kate, Thomas, and Meg—Thank you for choosing me to be your mama. So much of this story weaving is for you and our future ones...so that we might be free, whole, and connected. I see the divine spark in each of you and love you so much.

And for Quanita—for trusting Spirit and showing me the way. You have made an eternal imprint on me and mine, on ours. Thank you.

TABLE OF CONTENTS

Preface 1
Why This Book: What is the Current Situation 3
Waking Up: Our Individual Journeys
   of a Shared Bondage and Freedom 6
A Reframing: Co-Creating a New Yardstick 14
Soul Promise: Why Me? Why Us? Why Now? 20
What is the Innerground Railroad? 31
Why do we need the Innerground Railroad? 36
Overstory + Understory 41
Our Ancestors: On Whose Shoulders We Stand 45
Our Fire Stories 47
Our Water Stories 55
Our Earth Stories 63
Our Mineral Stories 68
Our Nature Stories 72
Integration 80
A 40 Day Journey
   The Integral Approach 85
   The Dagara Cosmological Wheel 88
   The Importance of Ritual 107
   The Overview 110
   Daily Activities 114-216

About the Authors 218

PREFACE

In this book Amy and I share stories because we believe that stories are the shortest distance between two people. Stories have been used since the beginning of time to share, teach, and bear witness to each other's journeys. We want to acknowledge the limits to this way of communication. First, stories live in us, so they aren't stagnant—as we grow and change so do they in us. We go back again and again revisiting what it feels like to us now and to dig a little deeper and mine the treasure that has been waiting for us to grow in maturity enough to comprehend the wisdom it has for us.

Individually, we are complex creatures. We live in a world that requires us to grow our ability to hold complexity. Complexity requires relationship to fully know and to be known. A diversity of relationships allows us to include as many truths as possible in our own assessment of what is true.

In this book, we are sharing our version of what is true to us in this moment of time rather than attempting to represent as many view points as possible to help you assess what is true. We are offering us, gifting if you will, our stories as we understand them to be in this very moment. Then we will guide you through your own stories. Holding close to our hearts the understanding that tomorrow these stories, ours and yours, and their gifts will be different even to us.

We also acknowledge that every person connected to our stories has their own unique version of truth that is just as valid and evolving as ours. We don't share our stories to discount theirs but to add our layer of truth to the world. It is our hope that as you read through each story offered you will find parts of yourself reflected in the spaces in between just as you are on that particular day in your own story.

We carry some assumptions on this journey that we want to make transparent from the very beginning. Below you will find them in no particular order.

ASSUMPTIONS:
- We are spiritual beings having a human experience.
- We are largely an adolescent culture in need of initiation
- Initiation offers something to us that we can't get any other way.
- We are stronger together than we are apart
- Every wound has a gift.
- The archetype of slavery shows us our way to freedom.
- The world is out to gift us, not get us.
- Everything is provided to restore wholeness.
- The external is a reflection of the internal.
- There are two energies in the world, love and fear.
- Fear can be an invitation to growth and healing.

It's also important to acknowledge the process by which these stories have unfolded. Quanita began writing this book about fifteen years ago. The two of us met three years ago and at that time it became clear that this book was being written between us. The evidence was the reality that I had already begun writing my part that, in many ways, was the mirror image of Quanita's. For example, our Waking Up stories were written before we even met! Over the years, as each of our stories came forth, we also paid attention to their relationship to one another, listening for what was emerging. These intertwined stories, are what came of this process of faithful listening and co-creation.

The art of story is a creative impulse generated by Spirit. Sacred process itself is healing, dynamically moving the authors between writing the story to being written by the story itself. Life has a life of its own and when we listen deep enough to what already want to be there is an ease that flows with the universe itself. We've seen this process as first about our own healing, we received many lessons along the way, many of them around surrender and trust.

WHY THIS BOOK?
The Current Situation

In the U.S., we are all swimming in the waters of what is right, real and true as White and male. Because of Western globalization, these beliefs have spilled over the rest of our world forming a yardstick by which we measure everything. Changing our beliefs, changes the yardstick. Changing the yardstick, changes the world.

What this yardstick tells us is that power is all external (what you do, who you know, what you possess) and that internal power doesn't matter. This yardstick values achievement over learning, independence over connection, power-over vs power-with, information over wisdom, dominance over relationship, control over surrender, certainty over trust, plans over emergence, doing over being, masculine over feminine, and White over Black. Running in the background, often invisible to us, this yardstick robs us of so much, mainly because it often excludes nature and spirit from the equation.

Stunting us, this yardstick stunts our growth, it tells us that our growth is achieved when we attain certain external milestones. Only by using this yardstick, of what is White and male, does what we understand as power and privilege make sense. By using this yardstick, we define who's powerful and who's not, who's privileged and who's not, healthy and who's not, worthy and who's not, wealthy, and who's not, successful and who's not, enslaved and who's not, and who's free and who's not.

This yardstick robs all of us of our power because it assumes power as external. Power from within is always more powerful; once you claim it, it stays with you forever. Power from without changes with circumstances. External power keeps us locked in the fear of loss—if it can be given from external forces, it can be taken away. External power seduces us into believing that security and freedom are based on something outside of ourselves, outside of the Divine. This belief conditions our lives as being *other-referred* rather than *self-referred*. Initiation invites us to step into our own self, it invokes self-actualization. Dependence arising from scarcity and fear, results in a state of co-dependency with others, blocking authenticity of self which keeps us from experiencing *deep interdependence* with others.

We've noticed that most recent conversations and movement around racial healing and justice today use the same yardstick, in yet another iteration. We, all of us, are still situating Black people and people of color as victim and White people as savior based on an us/them paradigm. For example, framing racism and White Supremacy as a "White people's problem", holds in place this notion that White people can and should set Black people and other people of color free, acting as if we are not all swimming in the same water. Freedom can never be given, because if it can be given, then it can be taken away and that's not freedom. Freedom must be claimed by each of us individually, Black and White, rich and poor, young and old and everyone in-between. Freedom cannot be bestowed.

We keep reproducing the same old systems and patterns because they are rooted in the same old beliefs. Until we get to and transform the root and heal the wound, we will continue to grow/create individuals, families, communities, organizations, and systems that are rooted in the wound. We will continue to recreate different iterations of what we already know. For instance, instead of standing for what we want, our calls for our systems to be anti-racist puts the emphasis on fighting *against what we don't want*, versus standing for what we do—which is always a weaker position of power. Because what we put our attention on grows, when our focus is on racism, we are growing it, versus centering our focus on healing and transformation. This is just another iteration of a journey we have taken before. What might it look like if all our energy is channeled into healing and transformation originating from a place of abundance and love, instead of focused on fighting racism from a place of fear and scarcity? What would it look like if that transformative process changed our core beliefs and the yardstick we use to measure, individually and collectively? What might that change look like in us personally and in the world?

Because we are spiritual beings having a human experience and not human beings that sometimes have spiritual ones, when we step away from reacting out of fear for what we don't want and instead respond with love for what we do want, we have an opportunity to step out of the cycles of slavery and bondage and into a lived experience of freedom and liberation.

The universe is only concerned with evolution and it always sends us exactly what we need for our own personal growth and soul development. But through the uninitiated eye and the old yardstick, the medicine that is sent to heal us can be seen as poison.

For example, the medicine that has been sent through the viruses of Covid offers us an opportunity to evolve, individually and collectively. After all, what better gift to send a world that has forgotten how to grieve than a pandemic? Because the universe is kind and because we have free will, the choice is always ours.

WAKING UP!
Our Individual Journeys of a Shared Bondage & Freedom

Quanita

"I think that we were the only family that I remember that called themselves Black. Everybody else was colored and most people were negroes, but we were Black. And I thank them, oh how I thank them for that, I'm so grateful. I'm not afraid of the dark." —Beah Richards

I am a dark skinned Black woman who was a dark skinned Black girl born and raised in Cincinnati, Ohio, the side of the river that represents freedom for so many, but not for me. The Ohio River for slaves was the finish line because crossing it meant freedom.

The deep brown tones in my skin reveal the stories of my 89% African heritage. It holds the secrets of the field slaves and hides the 11% European slave owner heritage that is buried deep inside. I don't assume that all of my 11% European ancestry wants to keep me enslaved anymore than I assume that all of my 89% African ancestry wants to be free. It's a complicated relationship as with most human stories.

This is a book about freeing the slaves. It's about transformation and liberation, it's about coming back to love, coming back home. This is my love letter to myself, to my African American brothers and sisters, and to a country that has yet to fully embrace me. I have been taught by my elders that the responsibility is always on the one most healed to go first because we can see more of the territory. Even though this is a love letter to us the journey is open to all, African American or not, American or not, because none of us are free until all of us are free.

I didn't know I was as lost as I was until one day I woke up and realized I was sleeping in the former maid's quarters of my house and my white husband was camped out in the master bedroom. The house was built in 1924 complete with quarters for the live in maid, a back stairway, bathroom and all. We didn't have a maid so I used this room as my coaching space most of the time and for guest when we had them. Our marriage was ending but the symbolism that this is, where I was while writing the InnerGround Railroad wasn't lost on me. Maybe I could finally allow myself to see it because my husband and kids were gone for the day. Maybe I saw it before but didn't want to admit it even to myself. How did I end up here? How did I end up in the maid's quarters of my own house?

I met my former husband when I was sixteen; at this point we had known each other for twenty-four years, had been married for fourteen, had two children, and survived the deaths of both of our mothers. I thought that all of that was evidence of love. Wasn't it? I had been sleeping on an old lumpy futon that doubled as a couch during the day for my coaching clients.

Standing in this room that has been infused with my own words about healing, I could hear them echoing back at me now. The responsibility is always on the one most healed, the only thing that can show up for you is what you are believing to be true about yourself, and what would you be doing if you were loving yourself?

Hearing these words sends this heat of rage through my body and I am caught off guard by the wailing that explodes from a place that I don't often allow myself to visit. The grief renders my legs useless and I end up back on the futon. Then it's as if all of a sudden my breath is taken away from me, I remember feeling like I couldn't breathe, like I needed to get out of there. I felt trapped and I wanted out. It's strange but in this moment there are two parts of me that I am aware of, the part that is very much out of control and the part that knows that I needed to stay there, I needed to let this, whatever it is play itself out. I needed to ride this emotional roller coaster all the way to the end. It felt like forever but eventually the ancestral rage gave way to the personal anger and I begin to take my former husbands inventory.

I begin to run through the list in my mind of all the things that were wrong with him. I couldn't believe I was here. No, Quanita, pull yourself together. Don't give this man anymore control over you then he already has. I just need to go. I just need to get out of here. Then I heard the voices of the women who have occupied this room before me, the former maids of this house, they said "be still, it is all in divine order." I tell them that it's not right, that I have been here long enough, it's his turn now. Maybe we can make a schedule and take turns sleeping back here until the divorce is final. They say it again, "be still, it's all in divine order. When you move back into the master bedroom you will take us in with you. You need to be here for now." This is not the answer that I wanted to hear. I am grateful and all for what they went through but this is too much. Didn't they already do this, so I didn't have to? Didn't they already pay the price? Why am I here now?

Okay, I might have to stay here in this room, but I can't stay here in this place. I won't, I know way too much to stay here. I know that anything that I don't heal gets passed on to my children and that is just not okay with me. So, I started the journey back to my bedroom, the master suite. It took a year and a half to get through everything that was blocking the way but I made it!

The journey wasn't predictable or easy. I had to face the fact that I felt unlovable and that I brought that bottomless pit into my marriage. I had to learn the difference between attachment and love. I had to grieve the fact that I chose a boy for a husband instead of a man because I was a girl instead of a woman. I had to forgive both of us for not knowing how to love ourselves and therefore not knowing how to really love each other. And most of all I had to stop making other people responsible for me and my happiness and learn how to take responsibility for myself, my life, and everything in it. So yes, I, "we" are going back to the master suite.

As African Americans in this country we don't get to live our lives as individuals. We are seen as the collective "we" everywhere we go. This "we" is simultaneously bonding and supportive and binding and restraining. Because of this I have a deep understanding that all of our freedom is bound to one another. All of our fates are tied together in ways we can't even imagine. This is why I need you, please come with me. I need to be able to bring my "I" (all that I am and all that I have been) to our "we" (all that we are and all that we have been) and I need to sit in the glory of your "I" in our "we" before I can truly rest. Until we all make it to freedom, there is still a part of the "we" that remains bound and restrained. Until all of us are free none of us are free.

That day in the maid's quarters I made a promise to myself and to you. I promised that when I did go back to the master suite I would buy us a king sized bed and I have. I prepared the space and there is room for all of us. The job of community is to remind us of who we truly are because we all forget sometimes. We forget how strong, beautiful, courageous and gifted we really are, we forget our truth.

There isn't a short cut to this journey; many have ended up in the master suite but it's not the same place without the journey. I'll tell you a secret that I didn't always know, others have already taken and completed the journey and each time one of us makes it back to the master's suite it makes a groove in the universe that makes it easier for the next person and the next person. The underground railroad is still in operation and is waiting for you. Join us. We need you.

Invocation:
I ask that the ancestors show up for each of us as we walk our own individual journeys. I ask that they guide, protect, and support us, that they let us know that we are not now and have never been alone.

Amy

I'm a White woman who lives on the Kentucky side of the Ohio River. The river that promised freedom to slaves, the river that traced the underground railroad. My life has straddled this river through childhood, education, marriage, motherhood, and work. This river, muddy and toxic and persistent, represents my seduction by empty promises of finally securing power and freedom somewhere "out there" in the world. It has taken my lifetime to understand that Freedom is not given nor can it be taken away. As a White woman who grew up in the South, this revelation has been a hard one coming, as it threatens all the lies and myths passed down. Tasting this revelation opens up a whole new way of understanding the world and my place in it. There is no going back.

I am choosing this Freedom, and in the perpetual choosing, awakening to the chains that have bound me. Waking up to these chains is painful and freeing myself from them is even more so. After all, they have held me together. Freedom then, comes in and through the falling apart. This is the story of this awakening and falling apart and what choosing has taught me about love, forgiveness, and surrender.

As I sit here, pen in hand with my dogs at my feet, listening to what needs to be said, I'm asking myself again why I'm writing this. Why do I feel so compelled to write this story? And why now? Honestly, I am not really sure. There is mystery here and I'm choosing to follow it, trusting. One thing I'm remembering is there is a deep knowing that exists that is all too easy to discount, dismiss, dis-member. When I do pay attention to the inner wisdom and listen to mystery, beauty emerges. I am listening and here I am. Sitting with my journal, felt pen in one hand, coffee in the other, hair wild on a Wednesday morning...kids stirring for school...following mystery and wherever it is calling me.

My trust and faith in mystery is born from acknowledging its loss. When, how did I lose it? Where along the way had I turned my back and forgotten?

I'm sitting with my then fourteen-year old daughter in her therapist's office, tears running down my face. I'm feeling a deep well of grief, rage, and sadness opening within me as I come face to face with the truth of this moment: my own shortcomings as a mother, the cracks in our family foundation that I've so carefully laid, the refusal of my daughter to be who I want her to be. Just as I graze that truth, her therapist reads me aloud and whispers, "You have to let go of your expectations, Amy." Or something like that. What I know for sure is that it was the kind of simple, cutting insight that slices right into you and stays there...for years. I didn't like it.

Because although I had landed on the edges of my rage and disdain for my teenage daughter, I had not yet arrived at the root of it all: my own grief. Those expectations were spawned by disappointments and betrayals—by things done and left undone—that left gaping holes within me. Those expectations helped protect me.

The therapist's calling attention to these expectations brought defensiveness and I was stunned. She clearly did not know me! All the work I had done! The mother I was and tried to be! She didn't know that I was a trained counselor with years of trauma work, a master's degree in Women's Studies. A doctorate in Counseling. That I worked with college students in social justice...that I was trained. I knew better.

And yet, there was something about the whispered insight that invited me to be present to those gaping holes within me and wonder, what if this "training" has pulled me away? What if it has distracted me from wounds and served as band-aids when deeper healing was needed? What if I could get beneath the expectations to which I've blindly grasped—to the root—my own fear? My own unattended suffering?

And how do we get at that suffering? Especially when the conditions and systems we've created have been designed to do otherwise? Conditions so deeply entrenched in our ways of being and doing that mostly, the wounds remain invisible. Conditions seeded and upheld by structures of domination—White Supremacy, patriarchy, capitalism—that threatens our existence if we begin to tease these out, or question, or disentangle?

For these structures are calcified through our process of becoming, taking root deep within us. Overtaking and choking out our inner, abiding home. And are manifested over and over and over again in our schools, healthcare system, housing, government so that they operate as gears in a well-oiled machine, each compelling the other.

Sitting in that therapist's office with my angry daughter, how could I possibly know all of this? And before this very moment, how could I have recognized it in the months, years, leading up to this moment? How could I possibly awaken given all that was swirling around me in the moving waters of my life? A recent move, three children, a toxic work environment, career change, ailing parents, trauma care, a dying marriage...

Leaving the hospital and the therapist's office that day, returning to work, I could feel a crack widening within me where that clear-cutting insight had struck. I held it together through meetings and mindless conversations—it was a new job, after all. I had to hold it together. I made it "home" that evening and functioned on autopilot through dinner prep and homework and bath time and bedtime.

Finally, silence. To be with that widening crack and gently explore it. To be. I trusted my need to tend to myself. I found the poem that the therapist offered as I left her office earlier that day. Kahlil Gibran's *On Children*. I re-read it. The crack widened. I wept, my body shaking. I didn't fully understand why nor really cared. But I allowed this pain to begin to move, speaking a truth to me I clearly needed to hear. Pain not only as a mother but as a child who had grown into that mother. Embodying that hurting child, all the while. Here I was, in that moment, a mother-child. Weeping for all of me.

How does the trajectory from child to mother remain uninterrupted despite our good intentions to do better? Do differently? I wasn't ready to know it then, but this widening crack was an invitation for me to explore this question from the inside, out. It was not a new line of inquiry. In fact, I'd been circling around this very question through decades of study, scholarship, research, and practice—all of which involved a certain level of intentional self-reflection and critique. And yet, what was opening up for me at this moment in my life was an inquiry that was not intellectual. It was generated from another place entirely and I had no control. The crack eventually opened so vastly that it swallowed me up for years and in that process of falling, the new and the ancient emerged. But at that time, I was not yet ready. We never are. I went stiff and rigid in my protest...

until I learned about surrender.

Just around this time, I began reading Gloria Anzaldua's last book, *Light In the Dark: Rewriting Identity, Spirituality, Reality,* a story of death and creative liberation. Gloria's writings have been medicine for me since I was in college; I've returned to her Borderlands over and over and over again for wisdom and insight. Light From Darkness beckoned me and yet at the time, I was not ready. I opened it, tasted it, and in doing so, found the gift of Coyolxauqui, an Aztec goddess who was dismembered by her brother; for Anzaldua, this figure represents the creative process of transformation, the healing of the wounds. I received this gift and then set the book aside—for years. Gloria was accompanied by other spiritual teachers and elders who guided me in trusting my falling apart as part of the spiritual path home to my Self.

"Besides dealing with my own personal shadow, I must contend with the collective shadow in the psyches of my culture and nation—we always inherit the past problems of family, community, and nation. I stare up at the moon, Coyolxauhqui, and its light in the darkness. I seek a healing image, one that reconnects me to others. I seek the positive shadow that I've also inherited."
—Gloria Anzaldúa, *Light in the Dark*

A REFRAMING
Co-Creating a New Yardstick

The medicine that has been sent through the viruses of Covid and White supremacy offer us evolution. When we understand this and understand that the universe is indeed out to *gift us* and not to get us we ask different questions. The question of "Why is this happening *to* me?" changes to "Why is this happening *for* me?"

What we've picked up with the yardstick of what is right, real, and true tells us that we are solely responsible for our own success and failure. It offers us the lie of independence. We are all always dependent on each other. We breathe the same air and walk on the same earth. When we are standing in fear and lack it is co-dependence, and when we are standing in love and abundance it is inter-dependence, but always dependence. We do however get to be individuals. The world needs each of us to bring our gifts. The problem with the belief of independence is that it takes God and nature out of the equation and we believe it is a trauma response.

One of the ways we see this is in our response to Covid 19. The moment that nature showed her face, we were struck with fear. This fear revealed truths about our relationship with death, grief, community, Spirit, life, faith, surrender, and responsibility. Our response was rooted in our collective and individual trauma. Based in fear, it sent us into fight, flight, and freeze. In fight, we turned on each other, demanding either that others should wear a mask, or insisting that you have no right to require that of me. Pushing for the economy to reopen, what some might say was too soon. James Baldwin said, "we've made the economy our God."

With this yardstick, capitalism has become our God. In flight, we dove head-first into being busier and busier, moving everything online, and turning to our addictions out of avoidance. Not knowing that we can never outrun ourselves. Concentrating more and more of our focus on the external instead of the internal. In freeze, we have been paralyzed in our homes, afraid to even be with our families, leaving our loved ones to die alone, and moving our focus from how we want to live to being afraid for our own survival.

Our survival is none of our business. Trauma makes us think that the divine left us and that we are responsible for our own survival. This doesn't mean that we get to be stupid, it just means that tomorrow is not nor has ever been promised to any of us. Our main job isn't to simply stay alive but to find our unique genius in the world and use it in service. This is what initiation teaches us.

The universe is only concerned with evolution and its movements are exact. While we were in our fear response, the earth was breathing life again; the dolphins were showing up in places they haven't been seen in years, places that have become highly polluted were starting to see clear skies, and animals that have been pushed out of populated areas were free to roam neighborhoods. Choosing fear, our human response was different, and disconnected with nature and spirit. And so we received another opportunity: the universe is generous. When we don't listen, there's always another chance. As tragic as George Floyd's murder was, his gift to us as he was leaving this world was an opportunity to hear the universal call once again to wake up.

We have been in pain for a long time, we just didn't know it. Now, more of us have become present to our own pain. Not knowing how to tend to it, we are grasping for what we already know, but what we know is anchored in our old wounds. Amy and I have asked ourselves the question, "How do we shift our belief systems, our own personal yardsticks and in the process change the world?"

To understand the how, we have to understand what blocks us. In Bill Plotkin's book *Soul Craft*, he talks about the importance of initiation. He shares with us that the journey to Spirit is an ascending journey, a masculine journey. It's where the spiritual collective "We" exists. This is why we have more ministers and priests that are men. It's the place where we are one, where compassion lives, where our spirits meet, and where the collective sum is greater than the sum of the individual parts. He goes on to share that the journey to soul is a descending journey, a feminine journey. It's where the spiritual individual "I" exists. This is where the soul can meet itself. In this descent, initiation happens which allows us to reclaim our unique genius in the world. We believe this is just one half of the equation: this is the spiritual walk.

Our human walk, the other half of the equation, is just the opposite: the human collective "We" is held by the feminine. The human individual "I" is held by the masculine. Our job is to find balance between the human walk and the spiritual walk, and the masculine and the feminine. We can do this through initiation because initiation takes you through a healing process that gives you a new yardstick that is not rooted in the wound. What initiation asks of us is to move from being earth-centered and -led to being spirit-centered and -led; initiated adults are very clear about their purpose because they have met themselves at a soul level. There are a lot of initiations in our lives. The one we are referring to is the one that marks our transition from adolescent or adolescent-adult to initiated adult. In our country, because of a lack of initiatory processes, we tend to either call up initiatory processes through trauma or we just grow older without growing up, creating a culture full of adolescent adults. It is time to grow up.

To understand the idea of spirit-centered and -led versus earth-centered and -led, we can look to the chakra systems. Mother Africa gave birth to the original version; the chakra system that is most familiar to most of us comes out of India. The earth -led chakras include the root chakra, which holds basic needs: belonging, food, water, shelter. The sacral chakra that holds your relationships to others, work, money, creativity, and sex. The solar plexus holds your self-esteem and your personal power. The bottom half of the heart chakra holds your love for others. The spirit-led chakras include the upper part of the heart chakra, which is where you discover your universal love. The throat chakra holds your personal truth, your voice, and your choice. The third eye chakra is the place of personal intuition and the crown chakra is where you receive Divine guidance.

If you think of the chakras as an hour glass shape, with the heart chakra being the center of the hourglass, the narrowest place—the place where the earth

-centered and -led and spirit-centered and -led systems meet. This is the place of initiation. Moving from making decisions rooted and led in the earth chakras into making decisions rooted and led in the spirit chakras move us from adolescent adult to initiated adult. Moving to a place of being spirit-led doesn't ignore the earth chakras, we just don't lead and make decisions from that place.

Because the journey to Spirit is a masculine one, it needs to be balanced with the feminine. Thanks to patriarchy, it's lack of balance with the feminine has created a culture heavily steeped in masculinity, often showing up as toxic masculinity. This culture creates and upholds patriarchal systems that have blocked the spiritual journey to initiation. The feminine journey, the journey to the soul, also requires balance with the masculine. This is why spiritual guides are so important. Guides balance the nurturing and care of the feminine with the holding and protection of the masculine, offering much needed structure in the journey to the soul.

Because the ascending journey to Spirit is a masculine one and often led by men who are not always balanced with the feminine, we need to balance it with the feminine. What the feminine gives to the journey is a rootedness in the communal. Because the journey to spirit is supposed to be communal, it holds the collective "We". When the feminine is missing, the journey is not able to offer its full promise: to hold us all in true oneness. Because our spiritual journeys are often held in religious institutions that are often designed and perpetuate the same old yardstick, we have created a culture that blocks the spiritual journey to initiation.

 Crown Chakra

 Third Eye Chakra

 Throat Chakra

 Heart Chakra

 Solar Plexis Chakra

 Sacral Chakra

 Root Chakra

In an individualistic culture that thinks we can do everything on our own and carries the myth of independence, we have lost the understanding of the importance of spiritual guides. Initiation requires us to lean into the descent. This is a place of birth. Robert Bly talks about this in his book *Iron John*. He said, (about male initiation) "Every man needs to have two births, one by a female mother and one by a male mother (a nurturing man). Just as in the feminine journey spiritual guides are so important, balancing the nurturing and care of the feminine with the holding and protection of the masculine.

The old yardstick is based in dualism and measures all meaning in terms of either/or, setting up the binary in terms of good or bad; right or wrong; one or *the other*; White or black; masculine or feminine; spirit or soul. Because the yardstick is insufficient, so is our meaning-making. The binaries are not the problem. It is how we measure them; it is how we hold their relationship that is problematic. We need a new yardstick that allows for both/and, that invites the dynamic relationship between oppositional forces and allows us to hold both. After all, they are both one side of the same coin. The universe wants balance. The way to create this balance is to first generate a whole new yardstick; as we have said before, as long as we're using the same old yardstick, we will continue to get the same results, merely reproducing new iterations of the same old story.

Here's some good news!! The new yardstick measures in such different terms that it can be disorienting at first. The old terms of progress such as "no pain, no gain" are no longer relevant. The new measures are "deep", "fun", and "easy". Does it have deep heart and meaning? Is it fun? (This doesn't mean that it doesn't sometimes include intense work.) Are you enjoying what you are doing and who you are doing it with? And, is it easy? Is there flow? When things are in alignment, the external should be easy even when the internal is hard. In other words, asking ourselves, "is this deep, fun and easy?" offers a quick and yet powerful assessment of whether we're using the new yardstick or relying on the old one. Yes, there are growing pains in the growing up process. AND the universe is here to gift us, not get us. It supports us, meets us where we are and welcomes us, leaving spiritual breadcrumbs along the way. Our efforts to restore balance and wholeness is celebrated by the universe, who's been cheering us on the whole time.

And more good news! The new yardstick is wrapped in grace. There is no messing up, here. We get to choose. Free will is real and so no matter what we choose, there is love. Because the universe is conducting the symphony, she will honor our key role and keep the music moving. Each one of us is just where we need to be for this moment, for our personal and collective healing. No judgement, no comparison, no shame/blame/guilt. Just imagine the possibilities.

The "co-creation" of a new yardstick speaks to the inherently relational nature of growing up. The process is communal. It positions each sentient being in an active role in this beautiful life-drama. Unlike the old yardstick that was rooted in individualism and separation, this new (and ancient!) yardstick is rooted in connection and community. The yardstick is both the measure and the means by which to measure—it is both process and product. We cannot measure alone, we cannot walk this path alone. This is why it's important to have guides, this is why it's important to not go it alone. We need one another to make sense, to see ourselves wholly, to navigate the wild landscape of our lives.

There is no such thing as independence. We are all dependent all the time. The old yardstick tells us the the question is between independence and co-dependence but we would like to offer a new (and ancient!) yardstick where dependence is given, and the question is between co-dependence (from a place of scarcity and fear) or interdependence (from a place of abundance and love).

OUR SOUL'S PROMISE
Why Me? Why Us? Why Now?

Quanita

Cincinnati holds the history of freedom, but it also holds the history of betrayal because at any given moment you could be grabbed and taken back across the river. I have felt this in all kinds of subtle ways. This is the place that inspired Harriet Beecher Stowe's book *Uncle Tom's Cabin* and the setting for Toni Morrison's book *Beloved*. In Cincinnati, my city, the legacy of slavery still plays out today. We still have race riots about every ten to fifteen years; this has been going on since the 1800's. Cincinnati is where we are aware enough to have an Underground Railroad Freedom Center but not aware enough to know that there's something very wrong with polishing the floor of the slave pen that lives within. We can polish the floor all we want but the dirt, gashes, and wounds of that time still remain no matter how much polishing we do. We haven't yet figured out how to transform our communal pain, instead of trying to gloss it over or transferring it to the next generation. Hence the riots because un-grieved personal pain turns into anger and un-grieved communal pain turns into rage. It is therefore fitting that this book, *The InnerGround Railroad* would also be birthed from this place. But spirit in it's divine wisdom didn't stop there. Spirit sent Amy, a White woman from Kentucky to complete this book with me. How fitting that we, together, would be called to reconcile this pain. Maybe it's the universe's way of creating balance, of reconciling not just what is in us but also what has happened here. Maybe it's just my way of making peace with my ancestors and honoring and keeping my promise to them.

MY SOUL'S PROMISE TO THE ANCESTORS
I'm standing in this log structure, two story slave pen, or slave jail as it is called by the close-knit rural community in Mason County, Kentucky, built to hold slaves awaiting shipment to Mississippi and the West. There are eight small windows, and a 10-foot fireplace, shackles on the central joist that run

the 30-foot length of the building to hold the male slaves on the second floor. The female slaves stayed on the first floor where I stand now. The females are able to move about the pen so to be able to cook and clean for themselves and the men. Tears are streaming down my face as I hear their voices, "How dare you?" one of them yells out, "Don't you know what we went through?" says another "How dare you not be all that you promised? All you have to do is put one foot in front of the other; we did all of the hard work." Standing here, of all places I know what they are saying is true. I know that I haven't been doing all that I promised. I know that I'm not being all that I said I would. Standing here, looking at the bars on the windows, the shackles on the floor, the scratches in the wood and hearing the pain in their voices, I can only imagine how scared they were. I can only image how betrayed they feel by me now. I am standing in the slave pen in the National Underground Railroad Freedom Center, at the base of the Ohio River, where years before I was born, thousands of slaves crossed in search of their freedom. Standing in this slave pen now, I find myself still on that search and after hearing their voices I feel more pressure than ever to find my way.

Wade in the water.
Wade in the water, children.
Wade in the water.
God's gonna trouble the water.

My journey is about freedom, forgiveness, and reconciliation. This journey has provided me the space to learn how to forgive myself, reconcile and welcome in, those parts of me that I had cast aside as not being worthy, and in the process, reclaim my freedom. My hope is that as you walk your own journey to freedom, our journeys will provide a path, some landmarks and maybe even some comfort along the way. I am sure Harriet Tubman told the slaves who came with her; this is a long hard journey and not for the faint of heart but freedom is always worth it. I will say the same to you, this is a long, hard journey filled with pain, sadness, amazing insights and even beauty. This journey will bring you to your knees and have you jumping for joy. This journey, the journey to freedom will bring you back to life even when you didn't even know you were the walking dead. The journey to freedom is always worth it.

PRAYERS FROM THE ANCESTORS

"But I do remember how she used to take us children and kneel down in front of the fireplace and pray. She'd pray that the time would come when everybody could worship the Lord under their own vine and fig tree—all of them free. It's come to me lots of times since. There she was praying and on other plantations women was a' praying. All over the country the same prayer was being prayed. Guess the Lord done heard the prayer and answered it."
—Tom Robinson (Former Slave)

WHY ME

I can't tell you exactly when I started the journey, as far as I know I have always been on it. There was always some part of me that wanted something different, that wanted something more but I couldn't always tell you what that something more was. Maybe it was the part of my DNA that held the dreams and the prayers of the slaves, the part of me that knows that my journey to freedom isn't quite finished yet. The part that still makes my heart jump when I see the drinking gourd and that knows even though my body has made it to the north my mind and spirit have yet to reach their destination.

You might be asking yourself why me? Why should I be a guide on this InnerGround Railroad to freedom? I asked myself the same questions and the answer that has shown up is that I have been uniquely born and raised to do this. My mother married a White man when I was about seven years old. I was raised in his family as well as my parent's families. I went to the School for Creative and Performing Arts in Cincinnati which was founded in 1973 as part of the settlement of the Bronson desegregation suit against Cincinnati Public Schools. While I was there the school was under a court mandate to administer all their programs as racially balanced 49/49 Black/White. The principal would give what we called the "Race Speech" every year. It went something like this, "If you are a Black student in this school and you don't have a White friend something is wrong. If you are a White student in this school and you don't have a Black friend something is wrong." Years later I went on to marry a White man, who was born in Tennessee and raised in Kentucky, the other side of the Ohio River. I am also the mother of two amazing multi-racial children, a girl and a boy. One day my father-in law called and said about my daughter, *"Makayla is the daughter of the American Revolution and I have documented proof."* This call made me think, who am I called to be to mother these two souls, the son and daughter of the American Revolution and the Descendants of Slaves, all wrapped up in these two beautiful packages I call Jacob and Makayla?

How do I hold all of who they are and who they are called to be this life time? How do I honor both of their lineages? How do I witness them so that they never feel like they have to be invisible? What I discovered in asking these questions was that the answer can only be found in my own liberation, in my own freedom. This book, this journey, mine and the guiding of yours is a part of how I mother and honor all of who they are and who they have promised to be in this lifetime. It is how I step into my own personal sovereignty. It is my soul's purpose here on earth and therefor I model for them the way.

According to the Dagara Cosmology I am a water spirit. The medicine I bring to the world is centered around the emotions-grief, forgiveness, and reconciliation. I've heard people speak about the slave story in this country not being a reconciliation because you can't reconcile what has never been. I would suggest that the reconciliation needed is internal. We are all born whole and complete, but this legacy of slavery disrupts our sense of wholeness. The reconciliation needed isn't just external, it's primarily internal. But because spirit lives in the paradoxes and because we are spiritual beings and connected to each other, when we reconcile the internal the external is shifted.

Also, while on this journey I've learned that the place where the slave pen that resides in the Freedom Center is from, (Maysville, Kentucky) where my ancestors are from. This is where my acnestors lived, were enslaved, ran to freedom, fought in the civil war, and participated in the underground railroad. I have been to this place. I have stood on the site where slaves, where my ancestors were auctioned off. I feel connected, I feel called to be a part of the healing, there too. So, you see, this is my family's business, this guiding to freedom. This is and has always been my legacy.

WHY NOW?

I met Amy late last year. It seems funny to say that because in some ways it seems as if we've known each other forever and in other ways it seems like it was just yesterday. We met over dinner; a mutual friend decided that we needed to know each other; we agreed. I felt an instant connection and invited her to attend an upcoming program that I was co-hosting. It was a short meeting but she and our time together stayed with me, enough so that a couple of days later I invited her to coffee.

During this coffee meeting together, I invited her to be an apprentice in an upcoming leadership program that I was going to host. It is unusual for me to invite someone I don't know into my work, because the work I do requires deep connection and I feel the responsibility that comes with holding space for others. I would also add that I extended this invitation without talking to my cohost but something felt right. I remember telling her that it was time. During this conversation I mentioned that I was writing this book, The InnerGround Railroad. She asked with excitement, "When can I read it?" I told her we could talk more later.

Shortly after she said yes to my invitation and asked if she could read my book. I sent her the first twenty-five pages. About a week later she answered by sending me a piece of writing that she had already written titled The Journey of the Shadow Slave: Master as Slave. I cried. I cried because of what I was reading—because I could have written what she wrote. I cried because I was so grateful that I had learned to listen to spirit and invited her into deeper relationship. I cried because I was so enchanted by the generosity of spirit. I didn't even know to ask for someone to birth this book with me. I knew from the beginning that it wasn't a book for just African Americans but I was prepared to carry it alone. I cried because spirit's plans for me are always bigger than my plans for myself and I was so humbled and incredibly grateful.

I texted her that night and simply said, I think you are supposed to write part of the book. She wrote back, "Yeah. Me too." I was right; it is time; and we are the ones.

Amy

I grew up in Kentucky, a border state. Stories told of my homeland were that "we" were neutral when it came to slavery. Another piece of that truth is that Kentucky was a breeding state, where slaves were bred and sold off, separated from their families and the place they knew as home. Our state song, "My Old Kentucky Home" tells the story of a slave being sold "down the river", asking the woman to "weep no more" while set to a strangely upbeat, happy melody. The dissonance alive in the South is also conjured by Billie Holiday's haunting song about the history of lynching, Strange Fruit. Strange fruit, indeed.

The brutality that took place on the land where I've grown up has largely gone unacknowledged by my people, so that the pain and tears this land holds, seeps into our bodies and souls, an invisible cancer that eats away at us. There are different levels of awareness of the cancer and different levels of pain. We are all impacted by it, stunted by it. As long as the cancer remains invisible, energy and resources are wasted, channeled to what Wendell Berry names "the hidden wound". Like secrets that eat away at the sources, our unspoken pains and transgressions kill us.

My ancestors carried these wounds with them as they fled their homelands in Scotland, England, and Northwestern Europe to immigrate here. And we know the damage these wounds have done in this nation; hurt people hurt people. Waking up to these truths can be painful. What I've found more painful is our not-seeing, is our willful blindness—the fact that we've been choosing to live all this time, unawake. The truth that somehow, unbeknownst to ourselves, we have assumed the position of purveyors of half-truths that in essence reduces the humanity of those we love and ourselves. Why?

I've grown up with lots of stories from and about my ancestors, stories passed down from generation to generation. Stories crafted to elicit pride, legitimacy, a sense of "who I am." Often the telling of the stories would be followed with the invocation, *Remember who you are.* And yet I never felt the stories painted the full picture. They never helped me remember.

I got the sense the stories helped me forget.

And so, I never claimed these stories as my own. They did not belong to me. And I did not belong to them.

These secrets, lies, cancers exist on multiple levels, from the micro to the macro. Uncovering one level calls for the uncovering of others as they are all interconnected. The journey to freedom begins by looking within and excavating the lies we've been told and continue to tell ourselves—the lies we fight for and cling to because our life depends on them. Because of the pain of this excavation, no one really does this by choice—at least not consciously. And we cannot do it alone. This journey is terrifying and is full of uncertainty. The guiding light is within us and everything in our conditioned lives has been designed to dim this light. We have been taught to distrust our light. To fear it. To unlearn these teachings, uncover our light, and then to trust it in shining our way is quite a transformation. It is only the *inner*ground railroad that leads to freedom.

Whiteness lies about this journey. It gives us the wrong maps—like a GPS gone bad. Rather than seeing the treasure and knowing as within and between us, we are taught to look for this outside of ourselves, in external positions, possessions, property. Power and privilege are secured externally. Our worth is determined by our accumulation of things, based in the material world, drawing our attention away from the real sense of power: the infinite source of Life within us.

This costs us greatly. And we pay. I have paid. In our own dismemberment of Soul and Spirit.

Why Me?
My mother was adopted. She grew up feeling like she didn't belong, with questions about who she was. When she was in her fifties, she discovered another full biological sister who had also been placed for adoption. Together, they found their biological mother and father, and each of their children. Some were accepting of my mother and her sister; some were not. Their biological mother later died and after her death, my mother reached

out to her mother's children. Neither of them was aware of my mother's existence and expressed hurt and betrayal that their mother had kept this part of herself from them. *Kept this part of themselves from them.* They were not only who they thought they were. They were more.

My father has a very strong sense of familial belonging, with generations of family stories and heirlooms and history. My paternal grandfather was registered in the Sons of the American Revolution; my paternal grandmother, a member of the Daughters of the American Revolution. Family stories were definitive and were passed down to me as sacred Truths. Yet, as Quanita and I were writing this book, a thread of these stories unraveled. We were not only who we thought we were. We were more.

In and between these formed stories lives Robina Phillips. Like a river running through the course of our lives, Robina has shaped my family history. And more than the river, Robina has also been a bridge, allowing me access to all parts of my familial stories, to all parts of me.

Robina came to Providence, Kentucky from Tennessee at age thirteen, having just married. The story goes that she married when she was still playing dolls. She began working for my great, great, great grandfather when she was about the same age as my great grandfather and continued working for four generations of my family. Robina has seeped into our bones and marrow and into who we are, who I am. I never knew her and yet she is alive in me. I've known Robina through the stories passed on about her love, truth, humor. She stands as a fierce maternal presence, breathing life into me/us.

And while there is a deep connection and love for Bina in my family, there is simultaneously a strange disconnection. Gaps that feel so profoundly gaping that it would seem impossible to not see them. And yet, they go unseen. Years ago, in the midst of a family dinner I gently wondered aloud whether Robina ever shared a meal with our family. The surprise and tenderness that rose up to meet my question whimpered: *tread softly here.* Here, in this gaping hole that we dare not see, dare not touch. There are stories we tell and those we choose not to.

Leonard Cohen writes that "there is a crack in everything that's how the light gets in." Robina has been the light in a crack of our story that has revealed both other cracks and the truth of ever more illuminating light in the darkness.

According to the Dagara Cosmology, I am a mineral spirit. The keeper of stories. Mineral spirits convey energy that moves through us on the way to somewhere else; we help to remember where we come from and what our purpose is. We hold a deeper way of knowing than what can be known through rational thought. I bring the medicine of mineral, of remembering our stories so that we can be whole, belong to one another, be free. I'm the child of both these stories and un-stories. My life is at the cross-section of stories told and untold. I am both the thread that weaves and the one that unravels.

My Soul's Promise to Ancestors

My thread carries meaning only in and through the ancestral fabric of which I am a part. It's taken my lifetime to understand this, to begin to embody it. I've learned the importance of forgiveness, reconciliation, and unconditional love on my road to freedom; the joy and grief that comes with surrender. Here I am, because we are. My promise to the ancestors is to practice remembering, a perpetual process of gathering up all the pieces of our stories, offering the gifts we can, and awakening to those whose threads join us in the sacred fabric of all living beings.

Why Now?

In listening to the call and response of Quanita's and my stories, there has been an invitation to find our stories in each other's, and go deeper in our own healing. As Quanita says, "more than belonging to each other, we are each other." This is what the journey offers: a recognition that our journeys are different and the same. And when we embrace the reality we are spiritual beings having a human experience; we can open ourselves to much more complex and vast Truths, Truths that also reveal a common human/divine journey.

Why do our particular stories/story matter? **Why us?**

Joseph Campbell offered us the Hero's Journey; Maureen Murdock offered us the Heroine's Journey, both rooted in Eurocentrism and Patriarchy. This journey of the InnerGround railroad offers nuance to a Westernized understanding of spiritual growth, revealing a freedom that is always available to us, when we find our way home. As two women, one of us Black and one of us White, the path is revealed as one that is communal and whose journey/destination is not only for the purpose of our own personal healing but the healing of our communities, of our world. The unfolding of our stories of slavery and freedom at this precise moment in our nation and in our world is not lost on us.

According to the Dagara Medicine Wheel, we are water and mineral spirits. We will explore more of this meaning later but for now, as we touch on "why us, why now", it's important to highlight that as water and mineral spirits, the two of us offer gifts of reconciliation and healing along with and remembrance and story. At this time of global pandemic, economic depression, and climate crisis, as historical wounds of racialized trauma and imperialism are brutally exposed, the medicine needed in our healing is that of re-membering, of tapping our collective spiritual knowing. It is time to shed our censored family stories, passed down in the same way Western ideology has spread like a virus through globalization, creating a crisis of story with devastating symptoms of domination, separation, and violence. Our times call for stories held sacred by ancient and indigenous peoples—stories based on interdependence, mutuality, intimacy. We need to remember who we are so that we can re-member ourselves, our world.

Through the call and response of our personal stories, our storylines connect to the chorus of Life. This chorus calls us beyond the feminist mantra, "the personal is political" to a level of consciousness that embraces "the human is the divine." It is no mistake that feminine medicine is being called upon now. This medicine flows through, lifting-up reconciliation storylines around mother-child relationships. These storylines join in perfect harmony with the universal mother-child reconciliation story unfolding in this historical moment of this global pandemic Our Mother Earth has called all of her children to be still so that we can remember our interconnectedness and reconcile our relationship with ourselves, each other, and our Mother Earth.

The calling forth of the Divine Mother offers us particular medicine. The practice of motherhood enacted in and through oppressive social conditions bears scars, passing trauma down from one generation to the next, shaping our very DNA. What has been the historical impact of White women handing over the care and responsibility of their children to women deemed less than human? What has been the historical impact of Black and indigenous women who have raised up generations of White children while also juggling the care of their own? What has been the impact on generations of human children born into and raised in this world? What if we could imagine and practice a different form of mothering, a different way to be human and be in relationship? What if...

WHY US, WHY NOW?
Walking this path of the *InnerGround Railroad*, both personally and together, transforms pain passed down for generations that we've carried, both personally and together. Walking this path together—two mothers/daughters, one Black, one White, one woman on one side of the river to freedom, one on the other—we choose to not pass this pain down to future generations. We choose to be who our ancestors dreamed us to be. Bringing forth feminine energy and drawing on the Dagara Medicine Wheel—born from Motherland Africa—we walk the spiritual path which turns inward then spirals out. We invite you to join us. Because you're already here, with us.

WHAT IS THE INNERGROUND RAILROAD

Quanita

"I freed thousands of slaves. I could have freed thousands more, if they had known they were slaves."
—Harriet Tubman

The *InnerGround Railroad* is a journey to remembering soul and spirit. The use of the word *remembering* is intentional. We need to remember: to remember our history, our strength, our journey, ourselves and our spirit—because, for enslaved people and for the slave owners that enslaved them there has been an intentional and unintentional dismemberment of those things in our selves, and in our communities. During slavery, as Denzel Washington's character in the movie The Great Debaters reminds us "the plan was to keep the body strong and the mind weak." I would add that there was also a plan to keep the soul and spirit weak. In this journey to soul and spirit we will also be able to strengthen our bodies and our minds. In doing so, we can remember ourselves and reclaim our freedom. I (Quanita) have been coaching clients for about twenty years and in this time I've noticed how the legacy of slavery (no matter what race) shows up in their lives and in mine. I have witnessed the courage that it takes to step out of the old stories and into new ones.

A friend of mine was giving a speech on courage one day and shared that for the first time she noticed the word rage in the middle of courage. She went on to say that every courageous act has a bit of rage in it. What immediately popped into my head was something that I read years before in the book *Iron John* by Robert Bly, who says that anger is personal but rage is archetypal. This got me thinking, what if by definition courage is archetypal or communal as well? What if knowing this could help us to choose courage more often? What if the moment we choose courage and step into a courageous act we move from the personal into the communal? What if this is where we truly become one with ourselves and each other? Maybe this movement from our personal fear into honoring our collective truth holds the very nature of being alive. The word courage comes from the root word cor which in Latin means the heart. In James Hillman's book, *The Thought of the Heart & the Soul of the World*, he writes about three different philosophies of the heart. The first is the heart of our passions, the warrior's heart, the heart that radiates and moves us from within towards something on the outside. Next he writes about the physical heart, the blood pumping, oxygen moving, keeping us alive kind of heart. Third, he writes about the heart of our being, our personal truth, the essence of who we truly are, the heart that radiates from the inside out. I'm starting to believe that stepping into a courageous act honors all three of the philosophies of the heart—our external passions, the fire in our bellies and simultaneously honors the truth of who we really are; and because of this, I believe that courageous acts are healing for our physical hearts as well.

Harriet Tubman once said, "I freed thousands of slaves. I could have freed thousands more, if they had known they were slaves." This book and this journey are about freeing the slaves—about acknowledging that slavery wasn't just a physical condition but an emotional and spiritual one as well. There are still many of us walking around as emotional and spiritual slaves. This book and journey are about waking up to the fact that we are still enslaved. This book asks that we not only be willing to be courageous in the journey but also that we take a leap of faith—that we allow ourselves to trust the process and walk the journey even when it doesn't make sense to our logical mind. It asks that we follow our hearts and know that there are forces greater than our own that we can lean into for guidance. We live in a culture that tells us that we can't trust our hearts, we can only trust our minds, but it's not true. Our hearts are connected to a universal truth that could never be explained by the rational mind. This journey isn't an intellectual experience; it may be a journey that starts in the head because it's in book form but that's only the doorway. We can often use the head to bypass the trauma and slide into the heart. This requires you to trust us as your guides; trust this process as a way through, trust your own discernment in choosing this book at this time in your life and trust in the divine order of things. We hope you surrender to the stories in this book and let them work you in all kinds of good ways. We hope you surrender to your own stories and let them work you in new and expected ways.

The legacy of slavery shows up through intergenerational trauma, often being passed down from one generation to the next without being acknowledged or healed. We can see the evidence of this trauma all around us, in our failing school systems, in our prison systems that support mass incarceration (another form of reenactment of slavery), in the breaking down of our families, in the number of killings of people, not only by other people but also by our police, in the rise of White Nationalism and White supremacy, and in our individual and collective mental, physical, and spiritual death. The legacy of slavery and the effects of being enslaved are evident in our present not just our past; and if we don't act now, it's destined to be our future.

Trauma will always rise to the top. It does this because it wants to be healed. Often when it starts to surface we think something is wrong and quickly move to cover it back up. Only when we are conscious of this can we take the steps to be freed. Only when we are aware of how the trauma shows up in us can we step into a new way of being.

Chorus:
Follow the drinking gourd
/Follow the drinking gourd
/For the old man is a waitin'
/For to carry you to freedom
/Follow the drinking gourd

When the sun comes up /
And the first Quail calls
/Follow the drinking gourd
/For the old man is a waitin'
/For to carry you to freedom
/Follow the drinking gourd

This journey was originally designed to give my (Quanita's) community, the African American community another tool in healing but to also be used for others that do not have African American ancestry. As I have traveled on this journey the book has changed. Amy showed up with her own journey and the road became larger and clearer to me. That's how the journey unfolds: you start off on one path and then are taken on another.

One of the biggest misconceptions in America is that the gifts and wounds' legacy of slavery is only for African Americans, that the gifts and wounds from this experience are carried by us, and us alone. Slavery is brutal. Enslaving another can only happen when a part of yourself is also enslaved. Amy's story helped me to see that this journey isn't only a side-by-side journey, but a *two sides of the same coin* type of journey. We need each other to fully reconcile our history because we hold in our wounds the medicine for each other. A struggle in her is a gift in me. A struggle in me is a gift in her. Sure, we can get the medicine in other ways but ultimately this is a journey of love and forgiveness. This journey is also one of complexity and as we said before complexity requires us to include as many truths in our assessment of what is right, real, and true. Together this process can support us in stepping into an unimaginable healed future.

I've come across people who have a problem with me calling us slaves and not enslaved people. I want to be really clear here, the use of the word slave is very intentional on my part and is infused with the love I have for the journeys that our souls have agreed to take. I don't see the word slave as a negative or positive word. The word itself is quite neutral. If we look at the word slave as an archetypal pattern, with a light and a shadow we can get more of the gift of the wound of this experience. The shadow side of the slave archetype is being a slave to another person, a thing, or even an idea but the light side of the slave archetype is being a slave to the divine spirit within. The slave archetype teaches us self mastery; it is how we find our freedom.

On her webpage Susanna Barlow says, *"The Slave is not about the development of independence but about learning to be guided by an inner truth. The Slave is drawn into relationships where the lessons, gifts and challenges of the archetype of the Slave are played out. The Slave archetypes a two fold pattern, one of slavery and one of mastery."*

You are invited to step into your own slave archetype in all the ways it shows up in you. You are invited to make your own journey from slavery to freedom. If you have heard the first quail call then it's time for you to follow your own drinking gourd. Having made our own journeys, we will be the ole women waiting by the river welcoming you home.

If you want to go fast, go alone. If you want to go far, go together.
—African Proverb

In this book, you will accompany us during our own healing journey through the five elements of the Dagara Medicine Wheel. Later, we'll accompany you through your own journey to remembering soul and spirit.

WHY DO WE NEED AN INNERGROUND RAILROAD

Quanita

The prohibitive cost of denying Otherness could not be more crucial to the survival of the human race. Our mass refusal to face the "Other within" has engendered a regimen of sociopolitical atrocities, genocidal horrors and environmental devastations-a virulent storm of global proportions. Contrary to the tenets of foreign policy and social activism, a remedy for this aggressive pandemic cannot be mediated, legislated, or enforced at a global, regional, or municipal level; it can only begin at the root, within each individual (intra-personally) and within our nearest and most intimate relations (inter-personally). It is therefore in this small and most private of territories that the potential for a truly humane society begin. —Daniel Deardorff

We tend to approach the world through one of three centers: either from the place of the body (instinct), of the mind, or of the heart (soul). But wisdom and transformation only occurs when all three of these centers come together. When we are centered in instinct, we can only react from what has already happened, a place of the past, not the present. When we're centered in the mind, we are trying to predict the future, from what we currently know, still from past experiences. But when we surrender to and are centered in the heart, the center of our being, we are able to connect instinct, heart and mind. Only then can we allow ourselves to be fully in the present moment where true healing can begin. The center of the heart is the place of initiation. This is where we moved from being led by our earth centeredness and led to being led by our spirit centeredness. As we said before this is where our soul meets itself, where we move from being adolescent adults to being fully initiated adults. This is where we grow up.

One day it hit me. I was/am addicted to the drama. I love the energy surge that I get when the drama shows up. It makes me feel alive. When this realization came, I started to wonder when this addiction started. To get my answer I had to travel through my cellular memories to visit my ancestors. You see, during slavery, the only way that slaves could survive was to be emotionally shut down most of the time. Being emotionally shut down isn't living at all but it is what had to be done if you were to survive. One of the few times they knew they were alive was when the drama hit. The drama brought with it a surge of energy; it brought emotion back into their lives. So, my ancestors started mistaking the drama for living and they passed that belief on to their children who passed it on to their children and they passed it on to their children who then passed it on to me. We like to think that slavery was something that happened a long time ago but my grandfather's grandmother was born a slave, so for me it's not that far removed. But the wonderful thing about consciousness is that it brings choice. Now that I know the drama isn't real living I get to choose. I can work on my own emotional expansiveness and learn what real living looks like or I can stay in the cheap drama. The choice is and has always been mine.

This journey isn't just open for Amy and me, you can do it too. If you feel your heart racing when the stress of life increases then maybe you are also addicted to the drama. It doesn't matter how or when your addiction started, consciousness brings choice and choice brings inner personal power. If you are waiting to feel courageous before you make this shift know that it won't happen because courage is a choice and an action not a feeling. The feeling with courage is fear. So, you feel the fear, you choose and act with courage, and you build your strength to become more and more fearless. As Marianne Williamson stated, *the drama never truly goes away*. But by choosing when and when not to engage we can get rid of the cheap drama and step into becoming real men and real women. We can step into living again.

Letting go of the drama and stepping into who we really are is the journey. It is at its core about initiation, expansion, and about self-actualization. My friend, Dr. Chene Swart would say *it is about re-authoring our lives, letting go of the old stories and choosing new ones*. In that re-authoring we get the chance to *re-member* what has been forgotten, *re-store* what has been lost, *re-connect* what has been broken, and *re-convey* what is true. In the re-authoring of our stories, we can reclaim our personal power and step more fully into who we were always meant to be.

> "*Leaving behind nights of terror and fear*
> *I rise*
> *Into a daybreak that's wondrously clear*
> *I rise*
> *Bringing the gifts that my ancestors gave,*
> *I am the dream and the hope of the slave.*
> *I rise*
> *I rise*
> *I rise.*"
>
> —Maya Angelou

Amy

I am a child of Southern storytellers, born from a strong lineage of weavers of story. Stories have been carefully passed down from one generation in my family to the next, painting a portrait of who we are. As I grew older and more educated on the histories of human civilization and colonization, I found myself listening to the cracks within the storyline through a lens of critique and suspicion. Eventually, all I could hear was what was not spoken—the silence, the gaps. And so, I began to fill these gaps. My questions turned to damning answers and judgements. Why did I only hear nostalgic stories about Robina Phillips, a Black woman who had worked for generations for my family during a time of segregation and Jim Crow? Why did my family—many of whom were educational and civic leaders in the rural part of Western Kentucky—never speak of the impact of desegregation or the Civil Rights movement? Where did my people *really* fall on the side of justice?

For a long time, I wore these judgements like a badge of honor, as if my rejection of my ancestry evidenced how *woke* I was, evidenced the level of my social consciousness. As I confess this now, there is great sadness in acknowledging how much energy I have invested in becoming what Ram Dass calls *somebody,* feeling the cost of that investment in my heart, mind, and body. Underneath the judgement and othering of my history and myself, lies shame. Over time, this shame festered in these wounds and eventually grew infected, like sepsis, seeping into my bloodstream and overwhelming the life force that flowed within and through my whole being.

On my way to becoming *somebody,* I cast my people away. And with them, cast away parts of myself and my sense of connection to the web of life. *Somebody* is a lonely and scary position to occupy.

When I began this leg of my journey in the writing of this book with Quanita, likely the scariest part for me was the uncertainty of how to access the ancestors—*my* ancestors. How could I begin to claim them? Would they show up for me? How could I repair the rupture in my personal and our collective history that held me in this moment? How could I fully locate myself in this story of race as a White-bodied person? This fear was my invitation to lean in, listen, and wait. And what magic there is in saying yes!

Whiteness is a lie. Race is a lie. It is for real fake news. At the core of this lie is that Whiteness is superior and with this superiority comes power and privilege. With all the focus on privilege and advantages and benefits, why do we not ask ourselves at what cost do these privileges come?

In the days immediately following George Floyd's murder, my children and I participated in the Poor People's Campaign's vigil for Mr. Floyd, holding silence for 8 minutes and 46 seconds—the length of time he had a deadly knee at his neck. During this time, I wondered, what happens in a human that creates such disconnectedness that he could choke a man with his own body over nearly *nine minutes?* How does such hate take root in us? What has happened and is happening in White bodies that drains our humanity and compels us to *other*?

The understanding that Whiteness comes with power and privilege is true only in the material world. And even then, the truth manifests differently across dimensions of class, gender, etc. The power granted by Whiteness stops at the material; in fact, buying into this form of power robs all of us of a much greater power—the Divine power within.

There is a Hindu legend that tells of Brahma taking away Godhead from humans because they kept abusing it. Wanting to hide it to prevent its abuse, he asked a council of gods for ideas of hiding places. The gods proposed the bottom of the ocean, the tops of mountains, the skies—all places Brahma knew the humans would discover. Finally, it came to him. *Let's place the Godhead within them—they will never find it there.* And here we are.

There is a spiritual crisis at the heart of White Supremacy and all other forms of domination. We are all diminished by the lies of domination, by superiority. Remembering we are spiritual beings having a human experience is the key to tending to this crisis, offering a whole different way to freedom—the way of love. The *InnerGround Railroad* represents this way, a way that has been here all along, hidden within us.

This journey has led me to be open to and love all parts of myself including my people, my ancestors. Saying yes to the invitation of fear and leaning in, my rage at things done and left undone dissolves into grief and compassion. Where my ancestors felt external to me before, they are now more a part of me, living within me.

I am so much more than *somebody*.

OVERSTORY AND UNDERSTORY

Cloak of Wounds by: Timi Singley

*I have been wearing this Cloak of Wounds—
this veil of pain and suffering passed down from mother to daughter
from sister to brother
from father to son
from grandparent to grandchild.*

*It is the cloak of an Ancestral past sewn carelessly
with wounding words and hints of hurts;
stitched half-heartedly with loss and anguish,
desperation and rage;*

*tirelessly trimmed with guilt and fear.
Today I remove this Cloak of Wounds—*

*offering this cloak to the Water to be washed clean
of its fragmented flesh and bloodied bands;*

*offering this cloak to the Wind
to be blown free of lack and limitations
and the ancient dust of illusions;*

*offering this cloak to the Fire
to be smoked and burned
as angered abuse
rise to the sky
and become the ashes of the past;*

*offering this cloak to the Earth
to be buried with all the isolation and despair of my People.*

On this day
I take needle in hand
and begin to stitch a
New Ancestral Cloak—

A royal robe of Power and Peace;
of Undying Hope and Deep Faith

Today I reach back in time to wind threads of
Hard Fought Freedom
with the hand spun fibers of
Grace and Love.

Today I weave together Inspiration
Innovation and Imagination
with Community and Cooperation,
intermingling wide bands of
Compassion with golden strands of Forgiveness.

It is this new Ancestral Cloak
that I will wear from this day forward
and pass to my grandchildren
to their grandchildren
and their grandchildren

Today I will don the New Cloak so that our hearts will be healed
so our minds may be cleared as we dance in the shelter of our faith;
so my people will be restored
held only by
the Soul of Spirit.

African proverb: If you want to go to fast, go alone.
If you want to go far, go together.

Healing and initiation are a messy business. It's not something that we should or can go alone, contrary to popular belief. Part of honoring our own humanity is knowing that we need each other. This is the essence of the word Ubuntu: I am because we are. Often when we think of this healing together, we think of it in terms of affinity groups. But what we're offering up here is that there is more power in diversity and that even though parts of it may seem more challenging, the individual gifts that we carry as Black people, people of color and White people provide the medicine for each other's wounds.

Our cultures so often hold *dark/Black as negative/bad* and *light/White as positive/good.* We are offering both archetypes as light and shadow. The dark also holds the womb space that grows the seedling into being, the space from which we are all birthed and will return, the cover of night that protected the slaves' journey to freedom. Light can also be blinding and annihilating, empty and void of meaning. In the culture we tell White people that they are supposed to be perfect and people of color that they never will be. Both stories enslave us.

The journey to initiation and healing can support white people in sinking into their own wound and the messiness of being human that is required to connect with their own soul. The journey of initiation and healing can support Black people and people of color in embracing and claiming their own unique wisdom and power from their experiences. The wound and the medicine are two different sides of the same coin because the wound always comes with medicine. The inability to acknowledge either, keeps us stuck.

When we come together from a place of trust and authenticity, then we can be way-finders for each other on our healing journeys. White people supporting people of color in knowing that they can take up the space that they take up in the world; Black people supporting White people in being in the mess of being human and finding the way to sit in the wound—because the universe is constantly trying to create balance.

There is an understory and overstory for all of us: the *on the ground, in-the-trenches* version and the *bigger picture* version. The understory is the warrior walk that we each have to go through. It requires us to descend into the unknown, face all the hidden landmines, discover all the old core wounds, surrender all to spirit, finding the gifts hiding underneath the surface.

The overstory story is the wisdom walk. What prevents people of color from doing the wisdom walk are the ancestral wounds of slavery that have been handed down, with stories and beliefs that it is not safe to claim your unique genius. White people tend to cling to and grasp for the wisdom walk before they have completed their warrior walk because the ancestral wound of domination has handed them stories that their worth and power is determined by their conquests and saving. In this book we walk through our own journeys and offer a different narrative altogether: as a White woman, Amy's stories reflect her warrior walk. As a Black woman, Quanita's stories reflect her wisdom walk. We invite White people to sink into your warrior walk and invite people of color to embrace the wisdom they have acquired through their own warrior walk.

In doing your warrior walk and stepping into your wisdom walk, we invite White people to pay special attention to where you've avoided sinking into the wound that blinds you from seeing the Truth. We invite Black, Indigenous, and people of color (BIPOC) people to pay special attention to where you cling to victimhood that blocks and sabotages your own gifts.

~| OUR ANCESTORS:
On Whose Shoulders We Stand

We call in our ancestors and all those who have gone before as we bear witness to our journey—personal, familial, communal.

We want your support, we need your support.

We would not be here without you—all you've done and left undone.

We give you thanks and stand strong upon your shoulders so that we might offer strong shoulders to those who come behind us.

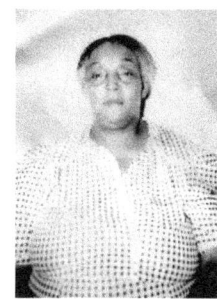

OUR FIRE STORIES
I BRING THE SPIRIT OF FIRE

The eternal flame burns in me through the voices of the ancestors guiding my every step
The eternal flame burns in me through the passion that pulls me towards that which I love
The eternal flame burns in me through the intuition that I carry and the truth that I speak
When my flame burns high you gain sight and understanding through the ancestors, through your dreams, and your own instinct

Quanita

MY FIRE STORY - PART 1 - FALLING IN LOVE
Sitting on the futon in my coaching space I prayed to fall in love with my life with reckless abandon. Looking back maybe the words reckless abandon weren't the best words to choose but at the time it spoke to something deep inside of me that was desperate to get out, to find a way to love myself, my life, and everything in it. It was my soul's cry. Looking back I know now that I had been dying inside for a long time and neither my then husband nor I noticed. Around the same time that I was praying this prayer I was also sitting with these three questions: What does it look like, feel like, sound like to love myself unconditionally? What does it look like, feel like, sound like to love someone else unconditionally? And who in my life was able to love me in that way? These questions were birthed in me when I witnessed a former youth volunteer of mine and his family walk through their own journey of learning about unconditional love. Questions are powerful. One thing about prayer and questions is that the moment we ask a question in prayer the answer is already trying to find its way to us.

Okay, so back to the original prayer to *fall in love with my life with reckless abandon*. I should also tell you that I was specific in my ask. I asked to fall in love with myself, my children, my husband, my work, and my house. I often want to do God's job and I want God to do mine, I want God to tell me what I want and I want to figure out how to make it happen. But that's backwards because we have been given free will. We get to decide what we want and then we have to surrender *when, where, how, and who* to spirit. This surrender is often very difficult because it requires us to let go at a deeper level.

Even though I didn't speak it at the time I think there was a part of me that believed that one day I wouldn't be in love with my life and then the next day (Poof!) I would—that it would show up in some magical instantaneous way—that I would be transformed all at once but what I learned is that it's not that way at all. First, love itself is magical. We don't know when or where it will show up. It is a gift from God.

The places where I thought I would find love often came up empty and then there were places where I would have never looked if left to my own devises. For me, love showed up in two ways. The first showed up as me remembering someone. I don't know quite how to explain it but until that moment I wouldn't have said that I wholeheartedly believed in past lives. I would, however, had said that I believed that love is the one thing that never dies; but I hadn't spent a lot of time thinking about what that really meant to me. I didn't know what that meant in real life, day to day experiences. Then one day I was talking to a friend, a person who lives in another country and whom I had known for about a year and I just remembered him—I remembered being married to him in another lifetime. I remembered loving him and what that felt like and I remembered him loving me.

Okay, this is where God has a funny sense of humor because remember I prayed to fall in love with my husband. I made the mistake of not making it clear that I meant the one from this lifetime. The memory came and left in a flash. It felt like 20 minutes had gone by but, in reality, it was probably only about 5 seconds. When you feel what it feels like to be loved, I mean completely loved, you are forever changed. Now, feeling loved is wonderful when everything is in alignment but there was at least one lifetime between those feelings and this moment. At this point I am still married and not to this person that I am remembering. My husband and I have been having some issues but at that time I would have said that I thought we would work things out. Before this moment I had never felt romantic love for this man. He was a close friend and colleague who worked for me. I would say it was an easy friendship. We fell into it as if it had always been and would always be. We both felt as if there was some work that we were supposed to do on this planet together—around forgiveness and reconciliation. When this *knowing the past love* happened I freaked out.

Once you know something, you can't not know it no matter how hard you try. What do you do when you remember someone? When you remember loving them, but you don't feel like you really know them? How do you hold another lifetime's feelings in this lifetime's reality? You might think I'm crazy. I know that I thought I was. I thought I had completely lost my mind. But there was a part of me that has always felt at home with him from the very moment we met, so even though it didn't make sense to my mind, it made sense to my heart; it made sense on a soul level. He felt like home to me. I still remember today what it felt like, to love and be loved. Thank goodness; what a gift! Now I know what to look for, now I know what to feel, so when it shows up I won't miss it.

The second way love showed up was in all these little moments of falling in love. How sweet is that! We get to choose each and every moment of each and every day to fall in love with what is right in front of us. I have a moment of falling in love with a close friend, while stepping into the deepening of getting to know each others hearts. Then falling in love with fireflies during a night walk in the woods, following the luminescent glow on the ground, in the bushes and high up in the trees. Falling in love with meeting Viola Davis for the first time and being able to tell her just how human and divine I thought her performance in Antwone Fisher was. Falling in love with hundreds of butterflies in a meadow filled with wildflowers at a retreat center that holds a special place in my heart. Or the magical journey of falling in love with the banana slugs on Whidbey Island. I never would have thought I would be enchanted by slugs. Before I knew it, I was in love with my life, all these moments strung together became my life. In Marianne Williamson's book *Enchanted Love*, she writes: *When we fall in love—with a mate, a child, or even an idea—a spontaneous enchantment occurs, a blessing that is ours for as long as we are capable of holding onto it.* This enchantment changes not only how we see the object of our affection but how we view everything. It opens up a portal to an enchanted world. It's as complicated and as simple as that.

Part 2

I was about eighteen thousand words into writing this book when my computer crashed. I wasn't worried about it then because we had a robo-drive in the house that backs up all our files on two different hard drives. It never crossed my mind that it was backing up every computer in the house but mine. I didn't find out for a while that the book was gone. All the work that I had done over the past five plus years was gone. I was devastated. It was all gone, all eighteen thousand plus words that felt like they had been pulled out of me. It made me sick to think about going through that process again. The journey had been incredibly healing but very painful. I didn't know if I could or even wanted to return to those places. For months every time I thought about the book I ended up in tears—until one day a friend asked me the most wonderful question. He asked, *What age does this book want to be written from?* At first I didn't understand the question but then he said, *See those books over there? They are all written from different ages. Some are written from an adolescence place, some from middle age, and some from a young adult. What age does your book want to be written from?* I said, it wants to be written from an elder place. He said, *That's what I thought! What age were the stories you lost written from?* I laughed and said they were written from an adolescent place. It was then that I realized that it wasn't that the stories I had written weren't supposed to be a part of the book, they just wanted to be written from a different place in me.

Sometime later I was sharing this story with a friend and she said, *Isn't that interesting that the book was taken away from you?* Something clicked. Taken away from me....I get it! The first walk through, the first eighteen thousand words were my warrior journey, it was my understory. It was me healing what needed to be healed in me. You see, we can't take someone to someplace we haven't been. I needed to do my warrior walk before I could guide anyone on theirs. The most amazing thing happens when we say yes to our healing journeys. There is a point in the journey where our old story, along with the pain that accompanies it, is completely taken away and replaced with a new story.

The new walk, the new story that was trying to be birthed through me was the wisdom walk, the overstory. The book wanted to be written from an elder place. I needed to go through the old warrior story because without it I could never have given birth to the new wisdom story. How amazing is that! The world is always out *to gift us* and *not to get us* no matter what it looks like in the moment, through our earthly eyes.

Amy

My freshman year at Saint Mary's College, I registered for a tandem course in *Anthropology and Literature on Ireland and Africa*. It was my favorite part of my entire first year. One day, my professor paused in class and directed her gaze toward me. In a tone both sugary-sweet and cutting, she whispered aloud: *Amy, you should consider going to a voice coach who can help train you out of your accent. You say smart things but you're hard to take seriously with your accent.* I choked.

If I were to become the *somebody* I aspired to become, this marked a new phase of my becoming that brought to light all the parts of me that simply could not stay. My Southern part, my White part, my Christian part—all were tainted, caught up in the web of domination and oppression. It seemed that to dismantle those systems, I needed to dismantle myself and disown these parts. I didn't realize then that on my way to becoming somebody, I cast my people away. And with them, cast away parts of myself. And with those parts, my sense of connection to the web of life.

Decades later, well into my *somebody* training, I asked Spirit to guide me back home. I wanted to find myself. The further I stumbled along the spiritual path, shedding the skin of *somebody*, the more the connections to *all of living beings* opened to me. The natural world, always a place of solace and restoration for me, held different meaning and a deepened relationship grew.

During a teaching with John Milton, elder and teacher of the *Way of Nature*, I had the privilege of spending time with the Sacred Land Sanctuary in Crestone, Colorado. This place has offered wisdom, spiritual awakening, and deep connection to countless spiritual seekers and Shamans for thousands of years. During this time, I was experiencing tremendous grief and a sense that I was falling apart. This grief was cracking me open and this time, I was choosing to not turn away. Well, ok—so what if it was a choiceness choice?! My grief had me in a choke hold and I had no choice but to surrender or die. I sat on one of the ancient stone meditation seats and during the time I sat, in communion with that stone, the cracks within me radiated my inner light to the cosmos in such a way that the skin of *somebody* broke wide open. Light and energy and life poured into and through me until there was no longer any sense of me at all. I felt like I was on fire. There was simply oneness. *Re-membering*. And what you know, you can never forget.

Just a month after saying yes to partner on this writing journey with Quanita, my father's side of the family gathered for our first ever family reunion in the Land Between the Lakes of Western Kentucky. My homeland. Returning there with them at this particular moment marked a way station along the pilgrimage to my unbecoming. In anticipation of this gathering, there was both anxiety and trepidation, as well as a healthy dose of good old-fashioned fear. Many years stood between us including life's tragedies and hurts—some of which were perpetrated by us, to us. Would there be forgiveness? Could we move on? Driving through the country roads that were both familiar and estranged, I found my way back to a piece of my heart I had extracted long ago. Opening my arms to these people—my people—both familiar and estranged, I found my way back to a piece of home within me that I had fled long ago.

As I stood watching my three children join with family they had never before met, I realized that my mothering had consisted of creating a nest for and feeding my young, preparing them for flight. At the same time, I had robbed them of the knowledge that we belong to a web of life and that migration is much easier in formation with our flock. I had robbed myself. My presumed shame and guilt precluded my ability to connect and take my position in the web of life, cutting short my ability to see in myself and my ancestors what Parker Palmer so beautifully names our *hidden wholeness.* Curiously, this shame and guilt and judgement kept me separate in an impossible box of *somebody* that made no room for me. The gifts and teachings from those who have come before me were blocked by the very walls I continued to build around myself. In a deep longing for ritual and ceremony and ways of knowing, I had no idea of how and where to access these lives, already within me.

Along this journey, I had spent a lot of time *trying*. I'd research people in my family tree, research the origins of my ancestors, sign up for classes and courses and programs and study groups. These all served me but did not give me the medicine I was looking for. At last I got it. *Stop trying. Relax. Surrender.* When there is relaxation and surrender into the present moment, there is magic. There is medicine.

Once, on retreat, a vision came to me: an indigenous grandmother was beckoning my *child self* to her. Her arms were outstretched and she sat, legs crossed, *Come, come, come.* I moved toward her and she embraced me, I melted into her and she swallowed me up into her belly whispering: *We are one. We are one. We are one.* After receiving this vision, I was overcome with this new truth and wanted to share with a witness. I turned to a friend and shared, tears streaming down my face. As I did, language pulled me back into the skin of *somebody*—I moved from my soul to my heart to my head and began hearing myself describe the vision and faltered. Doubt slipped in and my voice became smaller, drifting off—she, in her own wisdom and presence, caught me. *Do you feel yourself distancing?* Or something like that. And her noticing helped me stay. Stay in the moment; stay with my knowing; stay with Divine Presence. I was able to receive the gifts of knowing, loving, and becoming the other within.

Seeing our humble attempts of trying, fixing, solving, helping as *human* and honoring these efforts and then letting them go, allows for space. In this in-between space, there is simply being—full and rich and magical. This where I've experienced fire medicine—burning away the illusion of separation, and other, and unveiling the *Truth of oneness,* wholeness. *We are one, we are one, we are one.*

OUR WATER STORIES
I BRING THE SPIRIT OF WATER

*The Troubled Waters live in me as I bridge
   communities together*

*The Troubled Waters live in me through the emotions
   that float to the surface*

*The Troubled Waters live in me as I channel grace for
   forgiveness and reconciliation*
My Water heals and transforms with a gentle flow

Quanita

MY WATER STORY - PART 1 - COMING FULL CIRCLE

When I was fifteen, I went to court and filed charges against my stepfather for sexual abuse. Technically the state filed charges and I agreed to be a witness, but I was told by the prosecutor that it was up to me if they were going to pursue this case. They didn't have a case unless I was willing to testify in front of the grand jury. I remember taking the whole summer to decide what I wanted to do. In the end I decided to testify, and charges were filed. At the time I was still living with my mother and stepfather, so things were a bit tense.

Interestingly, I didn't make the decision to testify because I felt like he deserved to be held accountable, but I agreed to testify because I needed to know that even if no one else was able or willing to stand up for me, I would stand up for myself. There was a part of me that knew that I would die if I didn't do it. I needed to be worth it for myself.

I first testified in front of the grand jury, which after deliberation, indicted my stepfather who had pled guilty to the lesser charge of contributing to the delinquency of a minor. This process took months. And all that time we are all living in the same house. Right before we entered the courtroom for my stepfather's sentencing, the attorney who had been representing me all these months informed me that he wouldn't be joining me. He had to be somewhere else, so another attorney, a person I did not know would be in the courtroom with me. I was standing, alone, on one side of the courtroom with the prosecutor. My mother and stepfather were standing together on the other side of the courtroom as he was sentenced to serve ninety days on weekends so he could go to work during the week. So, the court decided that he would stay in the house with my mom and me during the week and go to jail on the weekends. I didn't realize until years later how traumatizing this day and the following couple of years were for me. As a matter of fact, I didn't feel much of anything. I was numb. I left the court room and walked to school and then later that evening I went home as if nothing had happened.

PART 2

Years later, when I worked at the American Red Cross. I found out that my grandfather (my father's father) had worked there years ago. It's funny how family cycles show up when you least expect them. During my time at the Red Cross, a young boy wanted to volunteer. My then manager walked around the building asking if someone could use Drew's help. I said I could. And so, twelve-year old Drew started working with me. His parents allowed him to work as many hours as he was able. Often he rode his bike to the office after tennis practice. (Drew and his sister's names are made up to protect their privacy).

Years later, as a young man, Drew contacted me and asked if I would go with him and his sister Leigh to petition the court. They were petitioning the court for early release for their sister, Anne, who had spent served seven years and a half years of a ten-year sentence for killing their mother. As I understand it Anne's plan had been to take her own life and her mother's. When I told Drew that I would accompany him to court, it hadn't occurred to me that the last time I was in a courtroom in this courthouse was more than twenty-five years earlier when my stepfather was being sentenced. I don't know all of what this day was like for Drew and his sisters. All I can share is what it meant to me. Being in that courtroom with them that day didn't just touch my spirit; it transformed me. It changed me forever.

The first thing I should tell you is that the court date happened to fall on the Monday right after the Connecticut Sandy Hook School shootings in Newtown, Connecticut. Drew's family's chance to petition the court was a one time deal. This was Anne's one opportunity to be released early. Anne could petition anytime between 5-10 years and she and her family decided that this was the time, of course not knowing that it would be the Monday after a school shooting. This was her one opportunity to be released early. If she wasn't granted release on that Monday, she would have to serve out the rest of her sentence.

It didn't occur to me where I was until my butt hit the bench. It wasn't until that moment that I knew something was happening, not just for them, but for me. I was sitting in this courtroom in the same building where I had been when I was sixteen years old—when I stood by myself, while on the other side stood by myself while on the other side of the room, my stepfather stood with my mother by *his* side, supporting *him*, instead of *me*.

I've said in the past, as a sixteen-year-old I didn't know that I was going to die on that day of sentencing. I didn't know that I would go into the courtroom as one person and come out as another. Years later, it's amazing to me how spirit will bring us back around full circle to experience how much we have grown or to push us the rest of the way through a block we don't know how to break through. By being there with Drew's family, I was able to relive my trauma differently—experience a sort of forgiveness and reconciliation of my own. Only this time the community showed up. It wasn't until then that I understood my sacred contract with Drew.

When Drew was younger, I was able to give him a place to go, a place that would in some ways save him. And, in return, he would come back one day, this day, and save me. Drew's sister's lawyer explained that the family could have petitioned the court earlier but they wanted to wait until they felt it was the right time. The siblings all had an hereditary eye disease and were slowly losing their vision. They wanted to get Anne settled before she lost her vision. The family recognized that many of the women who were released from prison end up reincarcerated, mainly because they didn't have job skills and found it hard to support themselves and their families. So, Drew's family took proactive measures to insure Anne's successful transition. They found grant funding to start a green training program in the prison which not only helped to improve the conditions that the prisoners lived in, it gave the women job skills.

In addition, a former neighbor stood up and explained that she knew if Anne was released the family planned to petition the courts to allow her to move out of town to where another sibling, Leigh, lived and in the meantime the neighbor and her husband would open their home to Anne. Then their Auntie walked to the front of the courtroom to speak and said: *I am here from India representing the grandparents and aunts and uncles on both sides of the family. We believe what Anne has done is morally wrong and she has started and will continue to make amends to her family and to the community. I pledge to serve as Godmother to her for the rest of my life.* When she was done a gentleman walked to the front of the room to address the court. He shared that he owned a business that built single family green homes in the city where Anne would relocate. He was prepared to offer her a job. He knew it might take some time before she would be given permission to relocate, he could allow her to work remotely until the move happened.

Tears were streaming down my face as Drew started to speak. The first words out of his mouth were: *This has been a journey of learning about unconditional love.* In that moment, these words threw me into my own journey in a way I have never felt before. He went on to say that for the past seven and a half years he and his sister have flown into town and driven 40 minutes for a three hour visit every month. He told the Judge that he had hope for the day that he and his sisters could go shopping together, and could eat a meal together. He then said something to the judge that I thought was remarkable, he said: *Whether or not you release my sister today, that day would still come, either now or in two and a half years, but I'm asking you to please release my sister.*

At this point I am sitting on the bench sobbing. The unfolding of this case in front of me cracked something open deep inside that I think was slammed shut the last time I sat in this courtroom. Drew's words about hope, his forgiveness for his sister and the surrender I felt from him for whatever was to come in that next moment changed me. Anne spoke and expressed remorse for taking her mother's life—that she learned early on in prison that talk is cheap. All she could do is use her life to make amends for what she had done and then she thanked the judge for his willingness to hear her. The prosecutor stood up and said: *It was nice that all of these people showed up but where were they when she killed her mother—that our system isn't just about rehabilitation but about punishment as well and that Anne could have gotten twenty to life but she entered into a plea bargain for five to ten years and she should have to complete the whole ten year sentence. She reminded the judge that he has never let anyone off early on a plea bargain and that he needed to be consistent in his ruling.* It just so happens that the judge was retiring that Friday and released her the next day.

I didn't know I was going to die again that day but I went into that courtroom as one person and walked out as someone different. I wouldn't quite understand just how much my life would change until later.

Part 3

About a month after the courtroom experience, I was driving home from my morning workout at the gym. It was 6am as I drove up to the house. I sat in the van in my driveway for a couple of minutes and then I started feeling what it felt like to be in that courtroom years ago with my mother and my stepfather. Feelings flushed through me—feelings that until then, I had never really felt it before. I wasn't strong enough when it happened so I just stored all of the pain in my body and now it wanted out. As I sat in my van, all of this grief started pouring out of me. The dam that had held it all in just broke. The final blow to it's foundation had happened just a month before in that courtroom with my former youth volunteer and his family. That was the beginning of the end. There was a part of me that didn't realize I had survived it. I had been carrying this trauma around with me, in me, for all of these years. I thought it was normal. It had become a part of the lens through which I viewed the world. I was finally strong enough to let it flow out of me. I was finally strong enough to feel it and let it go. I have said since then—that was the day I grew up.

Amy

When a tree is injured, it must seal off the wound and protect itself from fungus attacking its heartwood—the inner, older wood, beneath the sapwood. Trees, like all living beings, are wise in their healing. Even when fungus infiltrates the heartwood and empties out the tree, it can still stand upright. Empty and hollow and numb. And upright. When a tree successfully *walls off* and surrounds the injury by creating new bark to protect around the heartwood, it can still grow as long as other, uninjured companion trees grow alongside. But sometimes, in cold winters, old wounds act up. They call out for attention; they call for more healing. These wounds are unrelenting. Peter Wolhlleben, in *Hidden Trees,* writes: *Then a crack like a rifle shot echoes through the forest and the trunk splits open along the old injury.*

It was always, simply, a matter of time.

My family did not speak of our wounds. We walled them up and kept standing upright. Wounds are considered private, family matters. Even within our family, wounds are whispered in hushed tones, with lowered heads. Wounds are one thing. The silence of the wounds another. I find the silence to be most threatening.

My parents divorced when I was nine years old. One night, as my brother and I were watching *Dukes of Hazard*, my mother announced she was leaving and she left. My paternal grandparents arrived that night and drove my brother and me, along with our dad, to their home, in Providence, Kentucky. And the next day, my brother and I started school in our new hometown—he, in first grade, me in fourth. We never returned to our home, our town, our church, our school. Reading through my childhood journals offers strangely little insight into what was happening in my life, at the time. More is gleaned from what is not written than what my nine, ten, twelve, fourteen-year-old-self penned on the paper. Even as that little girl, hurting and so confused, I was learning and practicing the art of walling off my wounds, performing as if everything was ok—performing even to myself. Maybe mostly to myself.

Several years ago, when my marriage began unraveling, I created a shared google doc entitled, *Dear You* as a way for Michael and me to communicate. Multiple times a day I'd go to the document and capture my heartfelt emotions, seeking some understanding, forgiveness, reconciliation. We had both hurt one another deeply and to move on, there needed to be forgiveness to move on. Each time I returned to write, I'd see that he had not opened the document and I would then spiral into more reactive writing. One day, it hit me. In reality, I was writing to myself. I was suffering because I was not accepting reality as it was. I was so scared of what might happen to us, grasping so tightly out of attachment and fear, that I wasn't able to be in the moment—to be present. And so, I chose to let go of that attachment and to lean into the fear. I redirected my writing from Michael to my *Self,* renaming the document, *Dear You, Dear Self.*

Dear Self became a mantra of sorts—an invitation to turn my inner dialogue, well...*inward.*

Over time, I began to notice that this tendency to seek external validation extended far beyond my marriage. In fact, there was a pattern of addressing my life story to the world—to others. In doing so, I was leaking out the power generated from within and prostituting it out to anyone willing to offer a smile, a high-five, a job offer, a Facebook *like*—and if the response was negative—a critique—a judgement—I'd get stuck and paralyzed, freezing myself in time. Even where there was no response—literally, *nothing*—I'd often create a response through my own internalized patterns of bias. On the road to *somebody,* I'd lost my *Self.*

In 1973, Wendell Berry wrote the *Hidden Wound,* a timeless story of how domination operates. It's the story of the Slave Archetype, illuminating how both the master and the slave are harmed by the paradigm of domination and the degree to which the master (shadow) slave must go to maintain the dominant position. There are deep soul wounds that result from the desperate attempts to be *somebody,* to occupy power, to gain privilege. These wounds have a cost.

In June 2020, Quanita invited me to accompany her to Maysville, Kentucky—the homeland of her ancestors and the site of a slave auction block. She had been asked to come to bring healing to the land, to the place, and to the people. In the days leading up to our visit, it became clear to me that my job was to stay present to the experience of the White-bodied slave masters, White women, and White children who participated as perpetrators of and bystanders to the violence enacted there.

When we arrived and set foot on that land, the energetic of the place was alive. It was striking. The people there had been investing in and readying the earth for repair. Quanita and our host were in conversation and I stepped away, tending to what was becoming present to me, in me. My steps were careful with intention, staying tuned into the white-bodied experiences. This was not easy. Whiteness conditions us to turn to Others—focus our attention there, on Black and Brown bodies. This White gaze is the weapon of domination. Now, I would not accept this impulse; rather, I kept re-turning my gaze, my attention to those White women ancestors who had stood by, with their children and participated in the dehumanization of other humans. Slowly, my body, tense and rigid, softened. My heart opened. Rage let way for grief and soul tears spilled down my face into that earth that held all of it.

I wonder nearly forty years ago, if the little girl had learned to write her life story as *Dear Self*...how might the story have unfolded differently? Reconciling that harm done *by myself to my Self* has been the greatest gift in the possibility of offering reconciliation in the midst of our suffering world.

᎒| OUR EARTH STORIES

I BRING THE SPIRIT OF THE EARTH

Mother Earth lives in me, in my walk, in my stance,
  in the holding of my deep roots

Mother Earth lives in me in the foundation that she provides
  through me for so many people

Mother Earth lives in me in my ability to create and give birth to the new
  When I shift the earth quakes

Quanita

MY EARTH STORY

> "Finally, we arrived home. When we stepped in the door. I knew everyone knew. The whole family was sitting around the dining room table. That was the first time I realized that this was a family problem, not a personal problem. All our lives had changed that day."
>
> —Patricia Roberson (My mother)

PART 1

When I was born my mother and father were 15 years old. I've been told that the day my father found out that my mother was pregnant with me was the same day he found out that he was accepted to attend an all-boys' boarding school in Michigan, Cranbrook. One of four children in his family at that time, he told me that was the first time he remembered considering the concept of delayed gratification. He decided that day that he could provide for his family more if he left and went to this school and became a doctor than if he stayed.

This was my dad's first call north-his first leap for freedom. I once told my dad that his decision to leave changed my life in ways he couldn't have known at the time. As he shifted, something in me, his unborn child shifted. My father had spent most of his early life in foster care and had recently been returned to his mother's house. Years later he said he missed his foster family, and it was hard to adjust to being back with his mom. I'm guessing that physical distance from his mother all those early years made it easier for him to leave home, made it easier for him to choose something different. I shared with my dad that one of his gifts when I was growing up was that I always knew, because of his choice, if I wasn't happy with my life, I had the power to change it. I also knew, even if only as a whisper in the back of my mind, that I could want and ask for more. This moment, his decision, changed everything. I often tell my coaching clients that one of the reasons that this healing journey is so hard is because the healing doesn't just happen to us. When we heal there is something that is healed in our ancestral line and in the generations to come all at the same time. Any pain not transformed is transferred. This is what it means to be connected.

It wasn't until much later that I discovered that the Underground Railroad Freedom Center slave pen that I had been standing in was from Mason County, Kentucky and the seat of Mason County is Maysville where my paternal grandmother's family is from. I didn't know as I stood in the slave pen that day that some of my ancestors may have very well been there. I didn't know that it was their voices I was hearing. I didn't know that it was them calling me home. I have since learned that the journey includes lots of moments like these, I call them spiritual bread crumbs. The ancestors leave a trail of them along the way so that we don't get lost and know we're on the right track. Our job is to pay attention, to look for these moments and let our souls be fed by them.

My mother was one of nine children, the sixth child born to a nondenominational preacher and his wife. When my grandfather found out that my mother was pregnant with me he stopped talking to her for weeks. One of my mother's sisters overheard her telling another sister in the bathroom that she was pregnant and told their parents.

My grandfather was already a father of nine and a grandfather of four. He couldn't believe that his daughter, this daughter would come home pregnant. He had such high hopes for her, she was always his favorite. She was smart, did well in school, and had one of the best voices in the church choir. He was sure she would make a great teacher someday.

When I was born I think I took a corner of my mother's place in my grandfather's heart. All the hopes and dreams he had for her were transferred to me. My grandparent's house was a place where the community gathered. My mother told me that the reason there were always extra people around was because there were nine of them, too many to invite over to someone else's house. So, if they wanted to see their friends it had to happen at their house or not at all. Except for when it was time to go to bed, the door to my grandparent's house was never locked, and there was always extra food on the table for whoever happened to be around at mealtime. Generosity wasn't something they did, it was who they were. One of the gifts that I received from my mother that continues to serve me well today is her generosity. She was one of the most generous people I have ever known-in that house-in that kitchen-it was slowly, over the years baked to perfection into her bones.

I believe that my mother and father really loved each other but one of the legacies of slavery is that we don't feel worthy of real love, and so often even when it is right in front of our face, we can't allow ourselves to have it. During slavery your beloved could be taken away from you without warning. They could be sold, gifted away, or even killed. We as a culture have played out this legacy time and time again without being conscious where it comes from in us, and without consciousness there is no choice.

My parents were best friends most of my childhood. They thought it was important for me to have both of them around, so every major holiday my dad would come and spend the night at our house so I could wake up with both parents there; even after my mom married to my step-father and my dad married my step-mother we spent holidays together. I believe my father assumed that my mother would wait for him. He was on his way to becoming a cardiologist and I think he thought she would wait for him to finish all of his years in school and then they could be married. She felt alone, cheated and abandoned. During her childhood her mother, my grandmother had several nervous breakdowns and at times didn't even know who she was. My mother decided then to never let emotions control her. The funny thing about stuffed feelings though, is that they become emotions that take over, sometimes without you even ever noticing.

Despite my mom's best efforts I found that her emotions dictated almost everything in her life. My mother was extremely intelligent-graduated first in her class, which is saying a lot since she had a baby at age 15. She felt left behind and trapped in a life where she never quite reached her dreams. My father did go on to college and then to medical school and became a doctor, a cardiologist. I often joke that I stayed in the family business. My dad works on physical hearts and I work on the emotional and spiritual ones. I never really knew how much they loved each other until I saw my father at my mother's funeral. He looked like he had just lost the love of his life. He looked like I felt.

Amy

"But, I need to say that no child should have to grow up understanding that his/her birth caused no much trouble for so many people that it had to be hidden. I understand that you were ashamed. I knew that I was a 'mistake' and that I was not wanted and so your shame was passed down to me. I have never really felt a sense of belonging. I've never known where I fit in. I've always felt like a stray dog that some very kind and loving people were willing to take in..."
—Elizabeth Stovall Anderson
(my mother, in an unsent letter to her biological mother)

My mother was adopted by an older Southern Baptist Preacher and his wife, a teacher, who were well past their childbearing years. She suspects her father took her in to please her mother and vice-versa while neither of them really wanted a child or wanted to be parents at that point in their lives. Her stories of childhood were those of never feeling a sense of belonging. And then, when I was nine years old, my mama left. She'd later tell me she did this for survival. My mother felt like she had to leave us with my father. She tells of having nothing to offer us. No family, no roots, no sense of who she was. She was looking for belonging, she was looking for home and she couldn't offer it to us until she found it for herself.

There's a saying that we are given the children we need. When Kate, my firstborn was about a week old, I was rocking her in the Cracker Barrel rocking chair that Michael had been gifted in his work with a moving company. Rocking my baby in this grand rocking chair conjured the precise image of myself I had always imagined: the good mother. My daughter could not have cared less about this image. Kate was screaming. I did the good-mother thing and remained steady. Bending down to her little, fire-engine red face, I whispered, "I will never leave you. However long you cry, I will never leave. I'll be right here. I will always love you." She kept screaming. I kept whispering...until it grew into a louder plea. Finally, I placed my inconsolable baby down in her crib, sweat dripping from my body. Immediately, she fell quiet, asleep. Peace. I can hear her now in her old little soul, "Back the fuck up, woman. I need my space."

Kate would have to keep teaching me the lesson of the importance of mothering myself, on my being clear on my own needs so that I could clearly see her's. At one week old, she knew those whispers were not for her but for the child within me. My daughter's needs were very different from my own.

When I was just about the age of my mother when she chose her own Self, the sound of a rifle shot rang out in my world as my hidden wounds split me apart—just like an old, injured tree whose wounds of the heartwood had not healed. The blood, sweat, and tears I'd poured into caring for others and the world hemorrhaged and with it, my sense of self. The truth was revealed that much of my whispers (and bold demands!) for healing and justice in the world, were also whispers (and bold demands!) to myself. And my wounds, knowing precisely how to finally get my attention, gently placed me in the position of my mother. I was gasping for life and was sacrificing the home I knew for one I wanted to know: the home inside of me.

Maya Angelou speaks it best: "You are only free when you realize you belong no place—you belong every place—no place at all. The price is high. The reward is great."

OUR MINERAL STORIES
I BRING THE SPIRIT OF THE MINERALS

The Ancient Minerals live in me
through the stories of those who have gone before
The Ancient Minerals live in me
through a knowing that seems to come out of nowhere
The Ancient Minerals live in me
through the wisdom that I carry in my bones

My Mineral runs deep and wise and connects the past, present, and future

Quanita

MY MINERAL STORY - PART 1
My step-father picked me up from school and drove straight home. He didn't say anything but this wasn't unusual; we often traveled in silence. I walked in the house and my mother called to me from the kitchen. I could tell by the deep slow sound of her voice that something was up. As I entered the room I immediately knew that something was wrong. She said, he told me. Thinking about it now, it's amazing that just those words and her tears told me everything. I don't ever remember seeing my mother cry before then. I was afraid and touched all at the same time. I was touched because I felt she knew my story in the way my heart felt it, there was a resonance that I felt with her in that moment. At that point I didn't know she was also a survivor, I wouldn't find that out till later. I didn't know what to say or do, I just stood there for what felt like forever waiting for her, waiting for her to protect me, waiting for her to kick his sorry ass out of the house, waiting for her to be/do what I thought a mother should be/do. But what she said in this quite sad juvenile voice was, *What do you want me to do?*

I was 15 and I didn't know. I just looked at her and shook my head. I wanted him to leave, but I didn't know how to say that in that moment. I didn't want to upset her anymore than she already was. A couple of minutes went by and she said, in a take charge adult voice kind of way, *I know what we need to do. We need to forgive.*

In that moment I lost my mother. I didn't quite understand how we got from what do you want me to do to we need to forgive, but those two things felt worlds apart. One minute she was the mother that I wanted. The mother that just heard this devastating news about her daughter, whose heart was breaking. The next moment she was in pure survival mode and I was invisible.

PART 2:
The day I picked up my mother's ashes from the funeral home transformed the way that I saw my relationship with my mother. Soaking in the bathtub, in the dark, tasting the salty tears as they ran past my lips, I was filled with grief- the kind of grief that hurts all the way to your bones. I was going to pick up my mother's ashes. There was something so final about that. But that wasn't the only thing that I was grieving, I thought that my mother chose him, my step-father over me. I didn't understand, being a mother myself, how she could have done this to me and then it hit me. That wasn't the truth at all, she didn't choose him over me, she chose him over her-she couldn't even see me. I wasn't even a part of the equation. Unhealed survivors are very selfish, because they are in the survival dance and not the sacred dance. They are reacting to life instead of responding to it. She couldn't deal with my abuse until she was willing to deal with her own. She was so afraid that she started to feel she wouldn't survive-that the grief would consume her. This is what trauma does to us. It makes us believe that God left us and then we think that we are responsible for our own survival. But it's not true. Our survival is really none of our business. Our survival is God's job and living is our purpose, or keeping our promise, as I call it, is our job. The healing of our trauma and pain means moving from the survival dance into the sacred dance.

Amy

I fell in love with Donnell when I was nineteen. He was a creative and a philosopher and a jazz musician. We met the summer after my first year in college when we both worked at the Smithsonian Museum in Washington DC. He was Black and Native American and made a point to claim both these identities. For my father, he was simply Black. And the fact that I was in love with a Black man was unacceptable. My dad had raised my brother and me as a single father. He was my safety and security and foundation. I loved Donnell and I loved my dad and I wanted to be accepted and loved by each of them. My father never accepted Donnell or my love for him, therefore, he could not fully accept me. I recall pleading with my dad that in many ways Donnell was more White than me. Looking back, I now see how harmful this was although my intention and plea was for my dad to see me. And he couldn't. I wasn't part of the equation. The storyline moved through me but wasn't about me. It was a storyline that had been passed down.

Maybe the power of my daughter's therapist's witness to me in the hospital that day to "let go of my expectations of her" was rooted in my own wounds around this. The storyline was moving through me, passing from me to my daughter and unless I took responsibility for this, the pain would keep spilling. I wanted to see and accept Kate. And I couldn't unless I could see and accept myself.

A few months after I met Quanita, when into the writing of this book, my brother and I traveled with my mom to Mayo Clinic as a last resort. The fact that we traveled during a blizzard seemed fitting. She was dying. And we were looking for answers, looking for life. Hunter and I were close and yet had spent very little time together as adults. I went away to boarding school at fourteen and we hadn't lived together since. Partnering in the dance of life and death for the next three weeks—through mom's second open heart surgery and cascading health emergencies—offered my brother and me a chance to know each other. We had nothing but time on our hands to share stories and make sense of all that led us to this precise moment.

Moments like this when a loved one is hanging on the line between life and death provoke reflection, grief, and reckoning. During this time, it struck me: the story we had both held our entire lives, the story that mom left was only one piece of a much bigger story. There were other storylines for which we needed to make space; there were other characters in the story and other things done and left undone. There was her full story; my dad's; their parents' and grandparents'. The single story that had rooted itself into our soul's heartwood, hollowing us out and holding us upright, was revealed for the half-truth it was. Being together in the caring of our dying mother and in tending to our own wounds, we could step further into the sacred dance.

The sacred dance invokes a creative energy that shifts all who participate. As one shifts, so too does the other. As we evolve, the stories that have brought us to this moment also evolve. Sometimes, we forget this and hold onto to old stories that in turn hold onto us and hold us back—from our purpose and from each other. The more we practice the grieving of old stories and create space for new ones, the more we grow our capacity for loving without condition. We come to know the power of unconditional love.

OUR NATURE STORIES
I BRING THE SPIRIT OF NATURE

The Playful Nature lives in me through magic that transforms and grows

The Playful Nature lives in me standing at the gates of all Rites of Passage

The Playful Nature lives in me as the trickster spreading joy and laughter

My Nature tosses aside the mask that you wear to unveil the truth of who you really are

Quanita

MY NATURE STORY: THE EVOLUTION OF THE INNOCENT ARCHETYPE
I can't tell this story without connecting it to my purpose and my background. I am the promise of forgiveness and reconciliation in the world. A big part of my work is about supporting the reconciliation and forgiveness of our ancestral legacy of slavery. To be able to do this on a global scale I have to be able to do it on a personal one first; you can't take someone someplace you haven't been. As I shared earlier I am an incest survivor. My step-father is a White man so a lot of my journey has been healing this wound, reconciling and forgiving this betrayal in my life. The way this has shown up for me has been through my relationships with the masculine.

LEVEL 1: THE NAIVE INNOCENCE
JASON—I believe in sacred contracts. Jason and I have one this lifetime. I call him my .5 child. I tell people that I call him that because his mother won't let me claim all of him, so I settle for half. I may claim half of him externally, but I carry all of him in my heart. Some people were just meant to have two mothers and he does.

Sabrina, Jason's mother and I have very different strengths and in this lifetime he has needed both of us. She and I joke that there are two different kinds of mothers, owl mothers-mothers that are a little more warm and fuzzy and eagle mothers-mothers who tend to take a sink or swim kind of approach to mothering. We believe every owl mama needs an eagle mama friend and every eagle mama needs an owl mama friend so our kids get everything they need. I learn so much from our relationship that it is impossible to put them all down here, but I will share a piece with you.

Sabrina was my college roommate. She and I lost contact for several years after I left Cincinnati and moved to San Diego. One night I felt the need to track her down which was easy with the internet. A couple of days later Sabrina was at my house introducing me to her then two year old son, Jason. Years later Sabrina was diagnosed with a mental illness. What a privilege it has been for me to be able to bear witness to her journey.

Sabrina and Jason live about four hours away from me. I was taking Jason home one day. This particular trip was very hard for both of us. Sabrina had just gone through surgery for cancer and Jason stayed with me while his mom recovered a bit. The whole trip home Jason kept asking why he couldn't stay. It was heartbreaking. He didn't want to leave his mom; that isn't what this question was about. It was more complex than that and I knew it because I had been there myself. I just kept reminding him that he had my number, and he knew how to get in touch with me if he needed me; but in that moment, we both felt that it wasn't enough. I dropped Jason off got right back into my car and headed home-crying all the way. I cried for him and his mother, who I knew was giving him all that she had. I cried for me and my mother. I cried for all the people who had to take me back. I so wanted them to save me. That night while talking to Jojopah, my beloved teacher-she asked me: "Who do you need to forgive?" I said: "all the ones who had to take me back. I just wanted them to save me." She then said: "They did save you. Do you know how I know? Because you are still here, and you are saving Jason. It just doesn't look the way you think it should."

Level 2: Innocence Betrayed
My marriage ended for me in 2010 even though at the time I wasn't fully conscious of it yet. Even though it wouldn't legally be over for another four years. I remember saying to a friend that there was a wave coming and I

didn't know if I could surf it or if I would drown, but it was coming and I knew it meant the end of the naiveté for my family. I just wanted a little more time here. My mother died. She had a heart attack in the middle of the night. I was her only child As I said earlier she was 15 when I was born so we were very enmeshed. I felt like I had lost my heartbeat and had to re-find it again. I was devastated. Who was I if I wasn't my mother's daughter? Those first couple of weeks I was in shock. I stayed in bed most of the time and just grieved. One night in an effort to find some relief from the pain I turned to my husband for comfort. I was trying to escape for just a little while into us. This was after we had already decided not to have more children. He'd already had his appointment scheduled for his vasectomy when we discovered that I was pregnant. He thought I got pregnant on purpose. He didn't understand that I was too much in my own grief to be that calculating. Evidently he didn't love me or know me enough to know I wouldn't ever do something like that not just because I loved him, but because of who I am in the world. I decided to end the pregnancy and felt alone and betrayed. For me this is when my marriage ended. This is when I decided that I was in this alone.

One thing that you should know about the innocence archetype is that for it to evolve to the next level it has to be betrayed. We can grow up within it. Even though I experienced lots of betrayals in my life none of them pushed me into adulthood like this one.

Level 3: Innocence Renewed

To illustrate what the renewed innocence looked/looks like in me I will share about my experience with four men with whom I've had close intimate relationships. Three of them showed up in my life while I was making the choice to leave my marriage. The first was my former husband. In my relationship with him I experienced a level of safety and security that then turned into my expectation in future relationships with men. Ironically enough that feeling of safety and security is what allowed me the space I needed to heal so that I could leave the marriage.

Next was the friend that I told you about earlier in the book that I remembered from another lifetime. I experienced safety, security, and a return of passion in my life with him, which became my new expectation. I knew then that I could have fire in a relationship with the masculine.

The third was a man who was my best friend for about two years. He is one of the most generous men I know. After my divorce he became home to me in a lot of ways. We loved each other deeply. I experienced safety, security, and fire between us, and he tended to me on a daily basis. This became the new expectation. I could be in relationship with the masculine where I was being tended to.

And last, I will share a bit about a brother/friend/colleague that I love and trust. He showed up in my life at a retreat the weekend I was deciding if I was really going to leave my marriage. He was, first the brother I never had and then a trusted colleague and friend, and now we are all of that and more to each other. I am learning to trust the unfolding of the journey with him. I am learning that I can stand in my innocence and vulnerability and trust my own discernment. I experience safety, security, fire, being tended, and also being met in my full power by the masculine through him. I think it's important to note that he is a White man, he lives in the United States but is Canadian. Through him I have learned that we are all in need of reconciliation with the toxic masculinity. Below is a piece that he wrote:

> *I am a man.*
> *A white man.*
> *A white straight man.*
> *Each of those realities means*
> *that I belong to categories for which there is shadowed*
> *history,*
>
> *abused power, and unearned*
> *privilege,*
> *that requires awareness and*
> *apology.*

However,
generally,
I won't apologize,
for being me.

When I am not merely
a straight, white, man
blindly perpetuating historical
injustice

I'm living with open heart
to evolve not just what I am
but also,
who we are together
in the new new.

—Tenneson Woolf

So, all of this has formed the new expectation in me, a new relationship with the masculine internal and external. I feel loved and cherished.

These deep friendships have renewed my relationship with the masculine, internally and externally.

Amy

The year I turned forty, I ran a marathon. The story I told at that time was that I wanted to run into my forties, embracing my age and who I was. Another piece of that story is that I was running away. The stories I had told myself about myself were no longer holding up under the pressures of reality. Things were falling apart. The life I had carefully designed was not holding up and I felt myself faltering under its weight.

At the time, I was doing campus-based sexual assault trauma response work and social justice education in an unworkable work environment. After months of escalating institutional tension against the backdrop of national activism around campus sexual assault, I resigned my job. And with it, a big piece of the identity that had served to define me for my entire professional, adult life. During this same time, my identity as a good mother was seriously challenged as I faced the reality that I could not save my oldest daughter from her anxiety and depression. Desperately seeking ways to bring peace and simplicity to our family life, Michael and I decided to move our family from Cincinnati across the river as he had landed a new job. We had hardly replanted our uprooted family in Kentucky soil when my father—at that point, still living in Western Kentucky—moved nearby. My brother also relocated from Washington DC to Cincinnati; at the same time, my mother was dying. In the span of a year, everything changed. That is, every external condition in my life changed.

I misled myself in devastating ways during this time of darkness; I fully believed that I was "doing ok", "being strong", "surviving" because I continued to maintain my disciplines and practices of running, writing, and time outdoors. I can hear my self-talk now: *Even now, given all of this, look at me!* In truth, I was so split from myself that my disciplined practices were serving to disguise my deep pain. What had once been my tools and practices of *self-presencing* had become strategies of *self-absencing*, distracting me from the harder work of simply being with myself in the throes of that darkness.

The day my daughter's therapist sent me home with Kahlil Gibran's *On Children*, I began to feel in my body that I needed to do something different to tend to the child within myself. But habits are hard to break. I had no idea of where or how to begin. My adaptive strategies kicked into full gear.

I have a vivid memory of around age eight years old. My mom had taken my brother and me to Lake Barkley beach, near where we lived. We'd go nearly everyday where I'd spend hours searching for pebbles on the shore, wondering why no one else was collecting treasure. Playing around in the lake, I had hoisted my brother onto my shoulders, proud to carry him. Proud to hold him up. There was a drop off and suddenly my feet couldn't touch the muddy lake floor; he was too heavy for me to hold and fear coursed through my body. We were going to drown. We were flailing and my brother was yelling. No one heard us. I'd catch a quick breath, sink down to the bottom, touch the bottom and propel us up and over...searching for another, higher level of the lake floor. Feeling the weight of my brother on my shoulders, the weight of the world, I saved us.

So, until now, in the falling apart, I had not yet learned what it meant to save my own self apart from saving those around me. And ironically, this was the very thing that was drowning me. As I flailed and fought to stay afloat during this life season, my writing served as both a keyhole into the darkness and the key that locked me in. I was stuck. I had deceived myself for months, for years, maybe for my whole life, as evidenced by my own words and those unwritten. I had been blind to myself, my pain, my heartache, my own *dis-membering*. All the while, believing that I was writing *my self* and not realizing that I was also erasing my *Self*.

During this time of uncertainty and darkness, having lost all groundedness and sense of who I was, the words of Pema Chodron struck a chord:

"The off-center, in-between state is an ideal situation, a situation in which we don't get caught and we can open our hearts and minds beyond limit... To stay with that shakiness—to stay with a broken heart, with a rumbling stomach, with the feeling of hopelessness and wanting to get revenge—that is the path of true

awakening. Sticking with that uncertainty, getting the knack of relaxing in the midst of chaos, learning not to panic—this is the spiritual path."

Could I simply stay with the shakiness? Could I simply be with myself?

I call it the choiceless choice. Yes, there is a choosing. And the only other choice is to depart this life. The betrayal of my writing-self left me in that lake, drowning alone without my lifesaver. And so, because of the gaping hole left by the grief and rage, I turned away from the writing to the healing of the writer. I learned to stay—to be in that shakiness—because I wanted the suffering to end.

It wasn't until I was consumed by my darkness that I faced my darkness. And in and from that darkness, I was both lost and found. I found my *whole self* there. I found the pieces that had broken away and been forgotten, the parts that were left still hanging on, desperately trying to heal. In the darkness, I found the light.

A couple of years later, I was on retreat in New Mexico. Walking among the Red Rocks, I tasted a profound fear. It was like a gut punch. Quick and clear and shocking. It woke me up and I knew immediately the fear I was facing was fear of myself. In that moment, I got a glimpse of who I was becoming, who I already was. This time, I knew not to flee, not to back up but knew that underneath that signal was an invitation to come closer—to enter that uncertainty with a humble knowing that the light within me was leading the way. Had always been leading the way!

The day after I returned from this trip, I met Quanita and she told me about this book. And so, it began: my befriending fear and trusting my inner knowing. Now, the writer could begin to write herself.

✺ INTEGRATION

"All I know for certain is that this is how I want to spend my life - collaborating to the best of my ability with forces of inspiration that I can neither see, nor prove, nor command, nor understand."

—Elizabeth Gilbert

I bring the Spirit of Fire

The Eternal Flame burns in me through the voices of the ancestors guiding my every step

The Eternal Flame burns in me through the passion that pulls me towards that which I love

The Eternal Flame burns in me through the intuition that I carry and the truth that I speak

When my Flame burns high you gain sight and understanding through the ancestors, through your dreams, and your own instinct

I bring the Spirit of Water

The Troubled Waters live in me as I bridge communities together

The Troubled Waters live in me through the emotions that float to the surface

The Troubled Waters live in me as I channel grace for forgiveness and reconciliation

My Water heals and transforms with a gentle flow

I BRING THE SPIRIT OF THE EARTH

Mother Earth lives in me, in my walk, in my stance, in the holding of my deep roots

Mother Earth lives in me in the foundation that she provides through me for so many people

Mother Earth lives in me in my ability to create and give birth to the new

When I shift the earth quakes

I BRING THE SPIRIT OF THE MINERALS

The Ancient Minerals live in me through the stories of those who have gone before

The Ancient Minerals live in me through a knowing that seems to come out of nowhere

The Ancient Minerals live in me through the wisdom that I carry in my bones

My Mineral runs deep and wise and connects the past, present, and future

I BRING THE SPIRIT OF NATURE

The Playful Nature lives in me through magic that transforms and grows

The Playful Nature lives in me standing at the gates of all Rites of Passage

The Playful Nature lives in me as the trickster spreading joy and laughter

My Nature tosses aside the mask that you wear to unveil the truth of who you really are

I BRING THE SPIRIT OF FIRE, WATER, EARTH, MINERAL, AND NATURE AND I AM MORE THAN ENOUGH.

OUR INTEGRATION STORIES

Quanita

"Denial is contagious and facts are an additive substitute for truth. All the fact-finding missions in the world cannot convince humankind to face this one troublesome secret. If only we gave credence to those half-heard whispers of the twin ravens who perch on our shoulders each morning. Imagine the difference in our world: contrary mysteries chattered in opposite ears, life and death, sun and moon, future and past, self and other, confusing the rational mind but reaching and informing a wholehearted wisdom. A different world indeed."
—Daniel Deardorff

I started this journey over 15 years ago. When the idea of the book first came to me, I didn't know enough to even write it. All I could do was write the outline of the book-like a down load I was up most of the night writing out the 40 days and what was behind each day. I had just started my Masters program in organizational development with a concentration in integral theory when the book came to me. That first night all that I knew was it was 40 days; it integrated the Dagara Medicine Wheel and the integral model.

Two years later, I was invited to a writing retreat and I needed to bring a project. I took my book idea out of the drawer. During this retreat I realized that I couldn't write this book without first writing my own story. Then a couple of days into the retreat it became clear that they weren't two different books.

Two more years passed. I had just gone through my divorce. By this time I had written over eighteen thousand words when my computer crashed and I lost the book. I was devastated.

A year later I went back to the writers retreat. This time it was clear that the ancestors voices wanted to be a part of the book.

Three more years and I'm introduced to Amy.

This book and my personal journey have been a process of co-creation. Along the way I've learned to listen to "those half-heard whispers of the twin ravens who perch on our shoulders each morning." I've learned that everything has a life of it's own and my job is just to pay attention enough to discover what it already wants to be, what it already is.

Amy

Today marks a year to the exact day that I asked Quanita to share her story of the *Innerground Railroad*. I had just returned from my retreat with the Guardians in New Mexico, where fear of myself greeted me and whispered me home. That journey began through the gateway of fear and leaning in has gifted me in abundance that is indescribable. Listening and following that whisper led me to ask Quanita for her story; share mine with her; say yes to co-authoring this story with Spirit through the bodies that Quanita and I occupy; say no to pieces that no longer serve with gratitude and love; and to welcome in parts of myself and my ancestors left forgotten and abandoned. It has brought me to the holy land of *my Self* and there, I continue to find the holy in all of life.

Miracles are everywhere. Not noticing them takes energy. And suffocates the breath out of us. Let us breathe.

Quanita and I recently spent a magnificent week in Wisconsin to birth this story. Much of the story was there, developing and growing in each of us for years. It was time for us to come together into deep time together to bring it out of us, into its new form. That week of birthing, birthed me anew. Here lies a story within the story to share. It could have fit in other places of my element stories. It belongs here, as the timing reflects the meaning of integration.

The second night of our arrival in Wisconsin, Debra—a Native American medicine woman and grandmother, who was hosting us—visited us. She shared with us a vision she had had of the slave ancestors standing on the other side of the lake, waiting for us—waiting for this story. As Debra shared this vision, my White-bodied and European ancestors called out to me at that moment and I felt them, felt their absence in this story of slavery and freedom. That night in my dreams, they returned to me. They were drowning in the lake, the Black and brown-bodied slaves still standing on the other side of the lakeshore, with my drowning people screaming out in desperation: *Don't forget us. Don't leave us behind. We want freedom, love, and forgiveness, too.* As I stirred from this dream, their voices ushered me to my awakening: *How dare you not be who you are. We have been waiting for you.*

This book and my personal journey have been a co-creation. It's been unlearning all the beliefs and behaviors that have separated me from my self and from others and learning how to pay attention and listen. And then, holding this inner drumbeat and finding the rhythms, finding how to join in the sacred dance with the universe that is much more alive than I could ever imagine—the dance of love.

A 40 DAY JOURNEY

"Believe me when I say we have a difficult time ahead of us. But if we are to be prepared for it, we must first shed our fear of it. I stand here, before you now, truthfully unafraid. Why? Because I believe something you do not? No, I stand here without fear because I remember. I remember that I am here not because of the path that lies before me but because of the path that lies behind me"

—Morpheus *(The Matrix Reloaded)*

Welcome to the forty day journey of the inner ground railroad, supporting and guiding you in the co-creation of in co-creating a new yardstick.

INTEGRAL APPROACH

During this journey, we'll take an integral approach to healing. By using the Integral Model by Ken Wilbur we can step into our healing from various directions. This model is often known as AQAL (all quadrants, all levels, all lines, all states, all types) and allows us to look at healing and our own experiences through these multiple lenses, giving us a more wholistic view of ourselves and our journey. Healing on a a personal level (or egocentric view), communal level (or ethnocentric view) and systemic level (or world centric view), this framework allows us to make our way through the journey. Because we are whole human beings and not compartmentalized people we need our healing process to be able to hold all of us. We need a process that is big enough to hold the complexity that makes up our divinely human experience—one that is able to make the shift to integration of healing not just an imitation of healing—to fully embody the change we need to heal.

We are giving you a very brief overview of what is underneath the questions and exercises in the The 40 Day Journey. We will share a small bit about the different parts of the model and how they are used in this book including the four quadrants: states of consciousness, stages of consciousness, lines of development, and types. The Integral Model is much more complex than we are going to speak to here because we aren't trying to teach you the model. We want you to know some of the framework underneath and the intentions of our holding.

THE FOUR QUADRANTS holds different aspects of the truth. The I quadrant holds the space for our intentions or the individual subjective truth. The WE quadrant holds the space for our culture or the collective subjective truth. The IT quadrant is where behavior is held or the individual objective truth. And the ITS quadrant holds systems or the collective objective truth. We tend to have our center of gravity in one or two quadrants often thinking that we are seeing the truth but we are only seeing a part of the truth. Asking questions from all four quadrants allow us to include more and more parts of the truth in our assessment of what is true. In a time of great complexity we are called to include as many parts of the truth as possible in our assessment of our current situations. The more we are able to grow our capacity, the more possibilities we are able to see and hold.

STATES OF CONSCIOUSNESS come and go, they are temporary. They allow us to move freely from one to the next, ever changing. They can include waking consciousness, dreamtime, deep sleep, meditative states and even what some would describe as trance states. During this journey you will have an opportunity to sit with and meditate on things. You may experience a deeper waking consciousness and/or a more active dream life. Trance states can be used to connect us deeper to ourselves, to others, and to spirit. Indigenous peoples knew/know how to use this mode of internal transportation as intentional healing. Because we live in a culture that often pathologizes things, we will find this unintentional shift into a trance state during traumatic times named as disassociation, reflecting today's trauma theories.

STAGES OF CONSCIOUSNESS are permanent marking our growth and development. Once you reach a stage of consciousness, you can access the qualities of that stage whenever you need them. Stages build on one another. For instance, in the Chakras system, each chakra is connected to the chakras below and above it. . In the stages of moral development, we move from me(egocentric) to us (ethnocentric) to all of us (world centric).

LINES OF DEVELOPMENT can include cognitive, moral, emotional, interpersonal, and spiritual. In this book we acknowledge that a person can be highly developed in one area of their life and have a low development in others. In our country we often make the mistake of thinking that a person who is financially successful or intellectually successful must also be high functioning in other areas of their life as well. This isn't always the case.

TYPE, the main typing system we are using in this book is the Dagara Medicine Wheel. We find the integral model to be a very masculine model and so the Dagara Medicine Wheel allows for a feminine overlay to the journey. You will find more on this wheel in the next section.

INTENTIONAL Individual Subjective I	**BEHAVIORAL** Individual Objective IT
CULTURAL Collective Subjective WE	**SYSTEMS** Collective Objective ITS

DAGARA COSMOLOGICAL WHEEL

During the journey we will be working with the Dagara Medicine Wheel Cosmology, a cosmological wheel because it tells of the Dagara's creation story. It helps us to discover why we are here and what we are here to do. As a foundation for our very existence, it teaches that we all have a place in the wheel; we all have a place in the world. Because this is true we all have purpose and therefore there are no disposable people. The Dagara Medicine was adapted for the west by Malidoma Somé, based on the spirit medicine from the people of West Africa in Burkina Faso. We have chosen to use this medicine wheel because of its connection to the African people and because this area on the continent of Africa is where I have been able to trace back a big part of my ancestral line. I have also chosen this wheel because it is from the area where my ancestors are from and I feel they have brought this medicine to me and me to this medicine.

I am eternally grateful for the Dagara people, Malidoma Somé and Sobonfu Somé for bringing this wheel and medicine to the west. I am also grateful to my teacher, Jojopahmaria Nsoroma for sharing this wheel with me. Over the years, Jojopahmaria has been many things to me. I met her on my first day of work at the Cincinnati office of an organization called Public Allies. She worked out of the Milwaukee office and this was her last trip before going on leave to care for her dying mother. The next time I would see her would be about seven months later at an all staff gathering. I remember three important things about that trip; one was that I was about seven months pregnant with my first child. During my time of being pregnant I felt more connected to God than ever before. During my pregnancy, the veil between this world and the ancestral world was thinner and I could feel it. There were things that I knew and felt that were clearer than before. Second, I said to her, "I have been waiting for you." At the time I wasn't sure why I was saying this, but I felt it so deeply it brought me to tears. Standing in front of her looking deep into her eyes I knew I had found someone, someone who I had to meet, someone who I needed to be connected to. And third, our staff was struggling with our executive director and had gone to the meeting to tell the national office that it was her or us. We were ready to walk out because we were having such a hard time working together.

The leaders of the organization, in their brilliance, called our bluff and instead decided to send in Jojopahmaria. She informed us that of all places, social service organizations should be compassionate enough and willing enough to take on the healing of their staff. So, she came and spent a week with us, teaching us about the Dagara Medicine Wheel, identifying our core wounds and exploring what was blocking us from moving forward as a team. During this week we talked about past jobs, family relationships, and hurt feelings between each other. We shared what we needed in order to move forward and we made a commitment to come together once a week for straight talk. Jojopahmaria was pure magic.

According to the Dagara Medicine Wheel she is a Fire Shaman and so she ended her visit with a fire ritual. This was a powerful beginning to a relationship that has now lasted over fifteen years. Jojopah has served as coach, mentor, teacher, sister, friend, and mother to me. I have learned so much by bearing witness to how she walks her own healing journey and will be forever grateful for her presence in my life.

There is power in combining yesterday's ancient wisdom with today's integral truth. Ukumbwa Sauti, an initiated Elder in the West African Dagara tradition reminds us, "These elements are in and of themselves powerful physical and spiritual entities that we are called upon to understand, respect and grow in deeper relationship with. This type of familial relationship with Nature is an integral part of our indigenous soul and the promise for our renewed connection to who we really are and to the Spiritual Power of Nature."

When I was first told I was a water spirit, I felt an immediate connection to the element of water. Water spirits are often very weepy as children because we carry the water, we carry the emotions. I was not only weepy as a child, but I am brought to tears even now at the drop of a hat. I remember my mother saying that all she had to do was look at me funny and I would start to cry; at the time I didn't know or see this as a gift. Water spirits are also the peacemakers, so we tend to not want to deal with conflict; as a matter of fact we try to avoid it because our purpose is to keep the peace. As I have matured as a water spirit and in my understanding of the medicine I carry I have come to value the importance and necessity of conflict as a tool for peace. Looking back, I can see that I have always been drawn to the water without consciously knowing that I was a water spirit. Now, after working with and reconnecting to my element I can consciously use, as tools these gifts of peacemaking, bridge building, and taking people to the emotional depth as tools in my healing work with myself and with others.

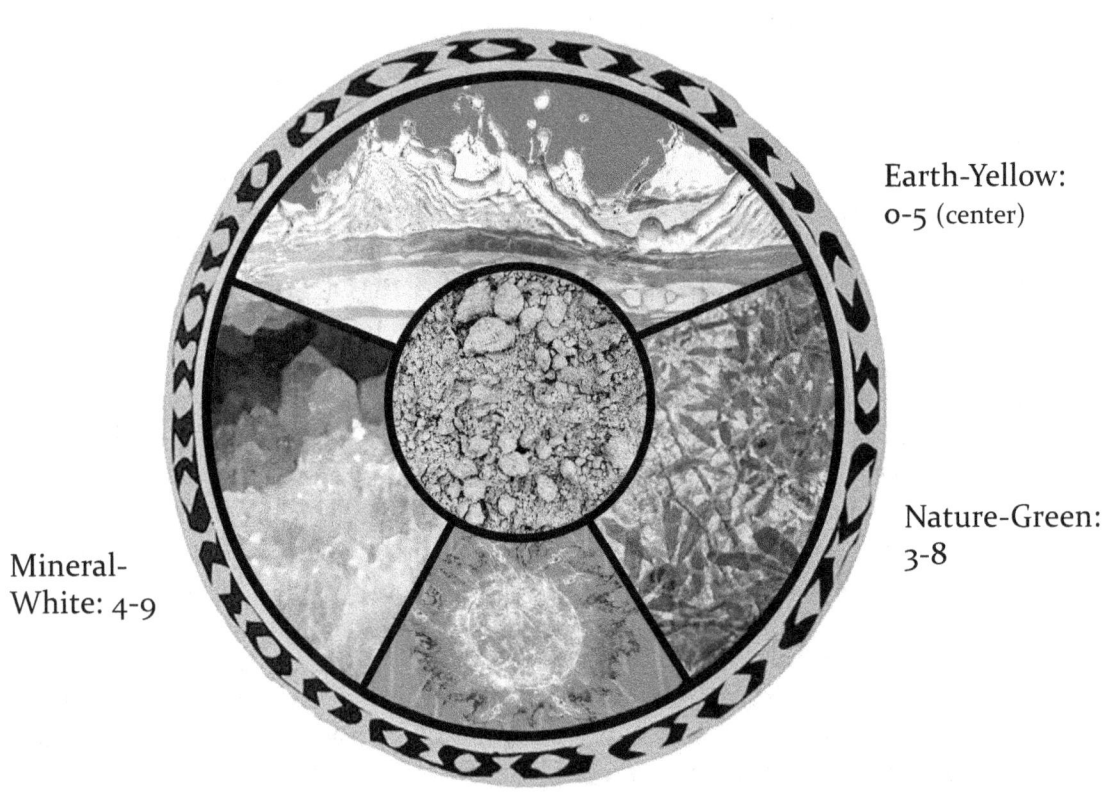

Water-Blue: 1-6

Earth-Yellow: 0-5 (center)

Nature-Green: 3-8

Mineral-White: 4-9

Fire-Red: 2-7

In the Dagara Medicine Wheel your personal element is determined by the last digit in your birth year. So, if you were born in the year of 2007, you would be a fire spirit; fire spirits have birth years that end in 2's and 7's. If you were born in the year of 1971, you would be a water spirit; water spirits have birth years that end in 1's and 6's. Below you will find a list of each element, the numbers associated with it and a brief description of each. These elements represent how you interact with the world. Holding the gifts you have brought to the earth through which you will fulfill your purpose. Each of us comes here with our own unique gifts, our own unique purpose. The wheel can help us discover both. It helps us to know we have purpose, to know that we are born knowing why we are here. The Dagara Wheel is also about community and about how each of these elements work together to create harmony, balance and fulfillment to create something bigger and better for the world. It teaches that it is the job of community to help support us in remembering that purpose. We each are born to a particular element but carry all of the elements within us.

Fire Spirits are the people who were born in years that end in 2 and 7
Water Spirits are the people who were born in years that end in 1 and 6
Earth Spirits are the people who were born in years that end in 0 and 5
Mineral Spirits are the people who were born in years that end in 4 and 9
Nature Spirits are the people who were born in years that end in 3 and 8

FIRE

Fire, ending in years 2 and 7 is associated with the dream world. Fire is the first element and primal energy. The Dagara's creation story tells us that in the beginning there was fire. There was a burning ball of fire in the place of our planet. Fire is in everything. It is associated with the emotional self, the intuitive self, the dream self, and the instinctual self. Its nature brings warmth and vision. Fire people walk a thin line between the ancestors' world and this one. It is the state the ancestors are in and where everything comes from and eventually returns. Fire spirits can connect us to the ancestors, they can open the channel. Fire people are said to live in two worlds this one and the land of the ancestors.

Dagara name for fire: VUN (voon)
Color associated with the element of fire: Red (Orange)
Position in the wheel: South

FIRE QUESTIONS:

- If you were born in a year ending in 2 or 7 take a moment to read and think about your answers to the questions below. Do they resonate with you? Do you feel connected to this element? Have you ever? You can record your answer in a journal if you want to be able to refer back to them later.
- Were you born in a year that ends in a 2 or a 7?
- Do you feel a connection to the ancestors or the spirit world?
- Do you remember ever being able to see spirits?
- Are you the one most likely to speak truth, to point out when things aren't quite right?

WATER

Water, ending in years 1 and 6, Water is life. Malidoma says "Water can lay claim to anything that is alive. Without water nothing can be purified, nothing can be authentic." Water is essentially about reconciling. Water can calm down the burning of the fire. Water helps to bring out our wisdom and can be used to bring things back into balance. Water can shape things over time or to move something quickly. It's about peacemaking and the building of bridges -between two cultures, between two people, or even two ideas. The creation story goes on to tell us that the fire collided with a huge body of water. This collision caused the fire to be chased to the underworld.

Dagara name for water: KUON (kwahn)
Colors associated with the element of water: Black and Blue
Position in the wheel: North

WATER QUESTIONS:
If you were born in a year ending in 1 or 6 take a moment to read and think about your answers to the questions below. Do they resonate with you? Do you feel connected to this element? Have you ever? You can record your answer in a journal if you want to be able to refer back to them later.

- Were you born in a year that ends with a 1 or a 6?
- Were you a very emotional child?
- Are you a peacemaker?
- Do you consider yourself to be a community builder?

EARTH

Earth, ending in the years 0 and 5, Earth was created as a result of fire and water coming together. Earth is about survival, nurturing, grounding, taking care of one another and unconditional love. It is about empowerment and providing a sense of home. This is where we find our identity and our sense of belonging. Earth is about rootedness, inclusion, safety, and security. This is the place of centering. Earth carries the energy of abundance and compassion. In The Healing Wisdom of Africa Malidoma writes, "Earth is the power to notice, to see and to thrill in being seen." Earth spirits want everybody to feel nurtured and content.

Dagara names for earth:
TENBALU (tehn-BAH-loo)/TINGAN (TEENG-gahn)
Earth color: Yellow (Beige, Brown)
Position in the wheel: Center

Earth questions:
If you were born in a year ending in 0 or 5 take a moment to read and think about your answers to the questions below. Do they resonate with you? Do you feel connected to this element? Have you ever? You can record your answer in a journal if you want to be able to refer back to them later.

- Were you born in a year ending in a 0 or a 5?
- Do you want others to be comfortable and have what they want?
- Are you one that more than not sees the glass as being part full instead of half empty?

〰️| MINERAL

Mineral, ending in the years 4 and 9, (Stones and Bones), is the storage place of memory. It is about communication; and the ability to converse. Mineral people hold the stories. In the indigenous world they are the storytellers. Mineral people convey energy that comes through them on the way to somewhere else. They are also known as stone people. Mineral helps us to remember where we come from and what our purpose is. Mineral holds a deeper way of knowing than what is possible through rational thought.

Dagara names for mineral: KUSIR (koo-SEER)
Mineral color: White (Grey)
Position in the wheel: West

MINERAL QUESTIONS:
If you were born in a year ending in 4 or 9 take a moment to read and think about your answers to the questions below. Do they resonate with you? Do you feel connected to this element? Have you ever? You can record your answer in a journal if you want to be able to refer back to them later.

- Were you born in a year ending in a 4 or a 9?
- Do you have a bowl of rock or minerals someplace in your home?
- Are you interested in the and tend to be the one that collects the family stories?
- Do you love writing or documenting events?

◈ NATURE

Nature, ending in the years 3 and 8 is about magic. It's about major changes- life, death, and rebirth. It's about dropping the masks and coming to your true self. It is about the coyote energy, the trickster, the joker. It is about joy and laughter. In Malidoma's book, The Healing Wisdom of Africa, he states, "The element of nature signifies the principle of change. It is transformation, mutation, adjustment, flexibility, cyclicality, life, death, and magic." The Dagara Wheel helps us to reconnect with our divine purpose and in doing so restores us with our community in a way that I haven't seen before.

Dagara names for nature: WIE (WEE-ay)
Nature color: Green
Position in the wheel: East

Nature Questions

If you were born in a year ending in 3 or 8 take a moment to read and think about your answers to the questions below. Do they resonate with you? Do you feel connected to this element? Have you ever? You can record your answer in a journal if you want to be able to refer back to them later.

- Were you born in a year ending in 3 or 8?
- Are you playful and do you love to joke around?
- Do you feel refueled by spending time in Nature?

DAGARA NUMEROLOGY
Feminine-Internal/Masculine-External & Positive/Negative traits

Written by Ukumbwa, the village na Wakale (and the Ancestors)

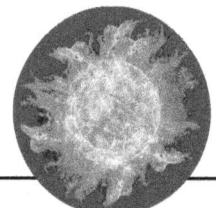

Vun - Fire

2 - Masculine / External
Positive:
- creative
- spark, catalyst
- dreamer
- initiates endeavors for/with others, gets things started
- passionate
- good connection to Ancestors
- gregarious
- inspires others to higher levels
- warrior

Negative:
- agitates others
- overbearing
- consumes too much, overuse
- over-production
- prone to anger
- over-emotionality
- craves negative attention
- restless
- allows others to be dominated
- dominates others wrongly

7 - Feminine / internal
Positive:
- driven by internal spirit
- finds inner inspiration
- strong dream life
- strong internal initiative
- self-motivated
- internally motivated
- stands up for self
- intuitive

Negative:
- passive-aggressive
- allows self to be consumed or used up by own activity
- internal combustion
- lives in dream world too much
- inner turmoil
- inner restlessness
- tortured spirit
- does not defend self
- too much of a dreamer

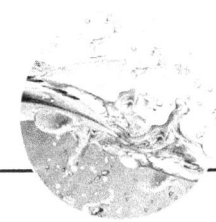

Kuon / Water

1 - Masculine / External

Positive:
- calming
- revitalizing
- peace-maker
- organizer
- unifier
- healer
- expresses emotions
- balanced expressions of grief
- brings life to community
- communal
- relationship orientation
- quietly persistent with people
- feeds/nourishes

Negative:
- takes too long
- ponders/considers too long without action
- focuses on larger issues and misses details
- doesn't express emotion
- allows people to rule them

6 - Feminine / internal

Positive:
- internally at peace
- clean, rejuvenated spirit
- can transform inner self/personality
- can change concept of self
- inner tranquility
- focused
- able to reconcile inner turmoil
- able to unify internal concepts and conflicts

Negative:
- inner agitation
- doesn't see/recognize individual gifts
- doesn't feel emotions
- cannot reconcile inner contradictions
- stagnant emotions/feelings
- emotional disorder
- dangerous to self
- does not renew self

Tenbalu/Tingan - Earth

0 - Masculine / External

Positive:
- giver
- nurturer
- takes care of people
- feeds people
- notices others
- makes others feel good
- conservationist, recycler
- good homemaker, nester
- shares warm, inviting home

Negative:
- uncaring
- over-user of resources/waster
- does not give enough/at all
- self-absorbed
- attention hog
- undercuts people's sense of self
- uses info resources against people
- hurtful
- closes off self/home to people

5 - Feminine / internal

Positive:
- able to nurture and develop self
- takes care of self on all levels
- recognizes own skills
- recognizes own identity
- can tend to self
- creates warm, inviting home
- strong self-identity

Negative:
- allows others to harm self
- poor home life
- scattered, ungrounded person
- no self-identity
- easily swayed to personal/ social action/thought
- battered spouse/partner
- misuses own gifts
- creates ungrounded/scattered energy in home

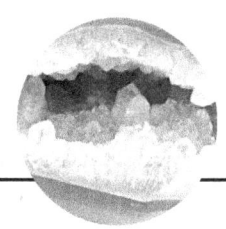

Kusir - Mineral

4 - Masculine / External

Positive:
- story teller
- remembers deep wisdom, purpose
- analytical
- good with words
- creative thought
- resourceful informationally
- uses symbolism well
- expressive

Negative:
- talks too much
- speaks from head, not heart
- likes to hear self speak
- lies to others, distorts messages
- living life/expressing self untrue to their purpose

9 - Feminine / internal

Positive:
- understands communication
- good listener
- good comprehension
- receives messages from Spirit world
- strong body memory

Negative:
- doesn't listen to inner voice
- closed to communication
- not able to hear from others
- not able to understand/comprehend
- lies to self
- doesn't get how life relates to larger concepts
- doesn't understand symbolism
- forgetful
- does not know purpose

WIE - NATURE

3 - MASCULINE / EXTERNAL

Positive:
- flexible
- understands system
- can create/set up systems
- magician/healer
- can create change/transformation
- pulls veneers away
- expresses authenticity
- speaks/lives honestly
- playful/joker/joyful
- shapeshifter
- witch/warlock
- lives an authentic life
- up front
- manifests for others well
- makes things come into creation

Negative:
- harsh with people/about them
- resistant to change/growth/development
- stops growth
- challenges people/ideas inappropriately
- subverts for wrong reason
- dry, too serious
- sullen
- unable to manifest ideas in world, manifests incorrectly

8 - FEMININE / INTERNAL

Positive:
- rolls with punches
- enacts personal change/transformation well
- honest with self
- can laugh at self
- manifests personal needs well
- able to transform own life/self
- makes self laugh

Negative:
- stagnant in self-development
- does not challenge self
- can't do for self
- resistant to change
- does not manifest ideas in own life

THE IMPORTANCE OF RITUAL
THE ACT OF SACRED SURRENDER

Quanita

Ritual simply put is a physical act of faith or a faith gesture. So often we get ritual confused with ceremony. Ritual is more than ceremony because it leaves room for the dance with spirit. It gives us the opportunity to practice sacred surrender. In ceremony each step is carefully planned out. Often there is no room for spirit to show up; there is no room for the unexpected. One of the things that I love about most African American churches is that they are filled with ritual. I once considered joining a Universal Unitarian church, but couldn't get past the music. I love all kinds of music, as I mentioned earlier, I attended a performing arts school. I was a vocal music major, so I've sung everything from classical Italian to jazz, to musical theater. Even with this background, I noticed that something was bothering me about the music. One day it struck me, the music that they were playing didn't leave room for spirit. It was so planned out that there was no room for the unexpected, no room for God. God shows up in the empty spaces. I once heard Sobonfu Somé, say: *The beat of the drum is the tuning of the soul.* I missed the beat of the drum. I missed the play with the congregation and the choir director listening to spirit with all of their being, listening to know where to take us next.

The power of ritual is that it invites in the spirit world; we can call on God, on the ancestors, on our angels and our other spirit guides to help us on our journey. This is ritual at its best. This is where this world and the spirit world meet. This calling on the spirit world is called an invocation. It acknowledges that we are not alone and that we have limited vision. It acknowledges that there are forces beyond ourselves that can influence our journeys in ways that we never could. When we call on them and ask for their help they show up. This is important. Because of our free will they are not allowed to intervene on our behalf without being asked, without being invited in.

Often, we will be asked to surrender something in this process-and not in a martyr kind of way but in a sacred way, that I have come to know as sacred surrender-where there is an offering to the spirit world with the promise of something greater. When my mother died I felt deep inside of myself the need to offer my hair. My locs were cut and offered to the fire in ritual. It wasn't until years later that I realized the gift that I received from the year I spent with my hair cut very short.

> *"Where ritual is absent, the young ones are restless or violent, there are no real elders, and the grown-ups are bewildered. The future is Dim."*
> —Malidoma Somé

Amy

When I was in college, I shaved my head and grew out the hair on my legs and under my arms. I had a need to somehow mark a transition in my inner sense of self, a shifting. In my women's studies courses, I was learning about female gender mutilation, arrested by Alice Walker's *Possessing the Secret of Joy* and her haunting invitation to explore what it means to be caught between two cultures, where ritual is lost and grieved. The absence of ritual resonated with me, although I had never named it in this way before. My life had been full of tradition, which felt very different from ritual and ceremony, which I sensed was more deeply spiritual, existing at the intersection of loss and gain, end and beginning.

Growing up, my brother, dad, and I went to church every Sunday. But the constraint of planned prayers from prayer books, routinized expectations of how to behave, and scripted hymns and music left little room for the creative and liberatory force of Spirit. I'd look. Always. As an acolyte in my little Episcopal church in Madisonville, my favorite part of the service was when I got to ring the bells just before communion. There was a precise place in the prayer, where the priest would pause for three—exactly *three*—chimes to be played. I'd relish in striking those chimes! That was about as bold as our service got.

I'd hear stories from my Black friends about their Black churches and my White friends about their Southern Baptist churches where Spirit seemed to move a bit more freely, through music, in the bodies of the church members, in the unscripted, soulful prayers to God. I was raised to revere God and church, to tread softly in the space and whisper softly, as if Spirit shouldn't be disturbed. Once, I recall standing next to my grandfather as we sang *How Great Thou Art*, struck by the tears streaming down his face; emotion was a stranger in the church services I knew. There was a hunger growing inside me for soulful experiences that would bring me closer to Spirit. And so, at this time in my life, I was staking a claim on who I was choosing to be, I shaved my head. But ritual is communal, a way of joining the fabric of community. Here, I was using it as an act of resistance, more of a statement of who I was not.

Becoming White requires burying *Power* for the sake of *power*. Whiteness is a myth based on the lie that worth is defined by dominance, an us/them, either/or paradigm. *To be White,* we must buy into and maintain this dualism, keeping us separate from Spirit, from each other. The myth of Whiteness does not allow for surrender; the myth of Whiteness rages at surrender out of fear of annihilation. Surrender to Spirit would mean the death of Whiteness, of ego. I choose to reclaim the roots of who we are—the essence of the sacred rituals and ceremonies that we've practiced before we became *White*. The rituals that invite sacred surrender, the *inner ground journey, and authentic community.*

A BRIEF OVERVIEW

The first three days of the forty day journey are set aside so that you can set your intentions. This is important because setting our intentions allows the journey to fold around you instead of you folding into the journey. Intention setting is tending to the soul: through the heart's courageous truth-telling, expressing it's true desires, the imagination comes alive and we dare to imagine a different world, a different possibility. This bold act opens the doorway for the soul to meet itself. When you stand in that possibility, it changes the journey—for the ego, the ethno, and the world centric. It allows an alignment of the head, heart, and soul—which changes everything.

Following the intention-setting, you will spend a week with each element. On the first day of each week you will have the opportunity to create an altar for the element you will be working with during that week. On the last day of the week, you will participate in a ritual associated with that element.

Days 1-3 are dedicated to planning and setting intentions. We will plan and set intentions for our body (egocentric or instinct), mind (ethnocentric), and soul (world-centric or connected heart).

Days 4-10 are dedicated to the first element, Fire. The primal energy of fire is associated with the emotional self, the intuitive self, the dream self, the instinct, and the ancestors.

Days 11-17 are dedicated to the element of water. Water is essentially about reconciling. It's about peacemaking and making bridges-between two cultures for instance, or between two people. It's also about bringing your wisdom out. Water is also where we find the emotions.

Days 18-24 are dedicated to the element of Earth. Earth is about nurturing, grounding, taking care of one another and unconditional love. It is about empowerment and providing a sense of home and identity. Earth is about vision, goal setting and abundant thinking.

Days 25-31 are dedicated to the element of Mineral. Mineral energy is about communication. It's about the ability to converse. Minerals hold the stories. In the indigenous world mineral people are the storytellers. Minerals store and convey energy.

Days 32-38 are dedicated to the element of Nature. Nature is about magic. It's about major changes - life, death, and rebirth. It's about dropping the masks and coming to your true self. It is about the coyote energy, the trickster, the joker. It is about joy and laughter.

Day 39 is dedicated to the integration of all of the elements.

Day 40 focuses on setting intentions on where you go from here. There's always another chance, another layer, another doorway.

The map of the journey looks like this, for both the WEEK and the DAY:

WEEK LAYOUT

Element of the Week

Poem to accompany week

A brief description of this week's journey and what the element has to offer for your healing.

Gifts of the Week
Elemental Posture - What it has to teach us

"Elemental quote from Jojopahmaria Nsoroma about the gift of the element ."

Here, you will also find a QR code to access elemental drumming that will support your journey this week.

Note: Each week will begin with setting up an altar for the element that you are working with that week and will end with doing ritual related to the element.

১ DAY LAYOUT

Quote of the day:
A quote to set a focus for the day and to root us in community

A list of questions to think about, ponder, and respond in your journal. You can do this a couple of ways. You could go through one or all of the questions and answer them by writing down your response in your personal journal or you could do it more as a collage in your journal, collecting artifacts, pictures, words from magazines, quotes, poems and thoughts that you have throughout the day that connect to the questions. This is your journey. Trust what works for you and know that it will be enough for now.

Activity:
Each day will have an activity that is rooted in healing an aspect of the element that we are working on that week.

Affirmation of the day:
Look in the mirror at least once a day and say this affirmation to yourself. It doesn't matter if you believe it or not, the universe doesn't have a sense of humor so anything we speak it takes as truth and starts to partner with us in co-creating it.

১ PLANNING AND SETTING INTENTIONS

1st Aid Soul Care Kit:
Before we step into our 40 day journey, find a box, about the size of a hat box. You can find one that is already decorated or you can decorate it yourself. This box will hold things that are soul feeding to you. During your journey you will be gathering up and making artifacts that you may want to come back to later. These things may become sacred items to you, having been a part of your sacred journey back home to yourself. Sometimes when life gets hard it is helpful to have a place to go that holds connections to a deeper part of yourself. I would also recommend that you get a journal to use on this journey. In this journal you can write your intentions, answer the questions for each day, and note thoughts, ideas, and blessings that show up along the way. It will serve as an archive of your healing journey.

Setting Intentions:
During the first three days of your journey you will set your intentions for the next 37 days. Intentions are so important because God has given us freedom of choice. Freedom of choice means that we always get to choose how we will walk our journey and a part of what we want our experience to provide for us. Every moment has what is called karma and creativity. Karma includes everything that has gone before; it is our history. Creativity is the ability to choose a different path at any given moment. These two principles live side by side. It is advisable to set intentions before starting any journey because then the journey can wrap around your needs and desires instead of you folding into it and handing over your own internal power to co-create. The universe always supports our intentions, conscious and unconscious. This is your opportunity to get clear with yourself and the universe about what you would like to get out of this journey. Know that setting intentions for this journey doesn't mean that there is no room for surprises along the way. When we leave room for spirit to show up it does. And when we are willing to see from the heart-mind (not the feeling heart but the imaginal heart) we gain greater perspective. Greater perspective opens us to more possibilities, more possibilities gives us expanded choice, expanded choice increases our internal power. Increased internal power allows for a deeper embodied co-creation with spirit.

As you work through your first few days of the journey you can use the first three pages of your journal to write your intentions. Having an individual page for each intention at the beginning will give you a place to come back and be reminded and to document when you have experiences that contribute to your intention.

Let's be very clear about our intentions for this book: our intentions are that this book breathes life into you. We intend for it to widen your perspective and help you to see what you haven't seen before. We believe that wider perspective = greater choice and greater choice = more internal power. By gaining more internal power, you are more capable of breathing life into everyone you meet and everything you do.

Day 1
Setting Intentions for your body (your egocentric self)

The body represents our egocentric view of the world. It is where we find our physical self. Our bodies allow us to experience the physical world in a tangible way. We are spiritual beings having a human experience. During this 40 day journey you will experience a shift in how you see yourself and therefore how you see the rest of the world. Our relationship to the world is just that, a relationship. We are half the equation so as we shift, our relationships shift. And we will begin to see things with new eyes.

Quote of the day
The body is a marvelous machine...a chemical laboratory, a power-house. Every movement, voluntary or involuntary, full of secrets and marvels!
—Theodor Herzl *(1860 - 1904)*

Journal Questions to consider on day 1:

Feel free to use any and as many of these questions as your writing prompt for today.

- What stories about yourself are held in your body and where in your body do you hold them?
- Do these stories support or block your connection to your higher self and what and what are the new stories you would like to invite into your life?
- Where in your body do you feel joy?
- Where in your body do you feel grief?
- What parts of your body are you grateful for and why?

Activity:

Find a quiet place where you won't be disturbed, where you can lay down or sit up straight. Take a moment to check in with your body. Give thanks to your body for all that it has done for you throughout the years. Consider this a practice of gratitude prayers. Start with your feet and work your way up your body. You could give thanks to your feet for holding up your body, thanks to your belly for carrying your children, or even give thanks to your eyes because they allow you to see how beautiful the world is. Take some time with this and enjoy the journey. Next, ask your body what it is that it needs from you, listen to what comes to you. Trust what you hear. Our biology holds our history, everything you have experienced on this earth you experienced in this body. It is constantly trying to communicate with us; we just have to take the time to listen. Honor what arises in your body as you set intention for this journey and capture this in your journal.

Affirmation of the day

Every cell of my body is happy, healthy, and whole.

DAY 2
Setting Intentions for your mind (your ethnocentric self)

The mind represents our ethnocentric view. This is where we connect to the communities that we are a part of. This view includes our families, neighborhoods, religious communities, ethnicity, and cultures. Our minds allow us to experience relationships with others. To be human means to be connected to others and this is where we first experience those connections. Ubuntu helps to illustrate this day. The definition for Ubuntu that we are using here is Ubuntu meaning "I am what I am because of who we all are." (From a definition offered by Liberian peace activist Leymah Gbowee.)

Quote of the day

Neo: What truth?
Morpheus: That you are a slave, Neo. Like everyone else you were born into bondage. Born into a prison that you cannot smell or taste or touch. A prison for your mind.
The Matrix

Journal Questions to consider on day 2:
Feel free to use any and as many of these questions as your writing prompt for today.

- How have the roles that I play in my communities shaped who I am today and how have I shaped the communities that I am a part of?
- Who do I want to be in the world, in my communities, in my family, in my work, and with myself?
- What are the ancestral wounds and gifts that have been passed down through my family?
- True and untrue, what are some of the stories I carry about my relationships?
- What would I like the story of my relationships to be?

Activity:

Find a quiet place where you won't be disturbed, where you can lay down or sit up straight. Take a moment to check in with yourself and quiet your mind. Bring the attention of your thoughts to the communities you are a part of and the relationships you have. Spend some time thinking about those different places, your family, your neighborhood, your church, your workplace. Who are you in these different areas of your life? Who do you want to be in these different areas of your life? Honor what arises in your mind as you set intentions for this journey and capture this in your journal.

Affirmation of the day

I have been born into a family and community that has the gifts and wounds that I need to fulfill my life's purpose.

Day 3
Setting Soul Intentions (your world-centric self)

Our soul represents our world centric view. This is where we find our unity with the world. This is where our purpose lives; in relationship to all. We have each been born to share our unique genius with the world. Dr. Clarissa Pinkola Estes says, "Your genius is the angel you were born with." This genius that only you carry is to serve the purpose of the highest good. It is something that only you can bring to the world. It is why you were born at this time, in this place, with these people. This is the place where we really can see that it's not all about us and at the same time it is. One day I (Quanita) was talking to Jojopahmaria and I explained to her that sometimes because I have been given so much, I feel that it is selfish to ask for more. She responded "That's just your ego talking because you think it's all about you. You don't understand that you having greater access means that you can fulfill your purpose even more." I understood what she was saying but it didn't really click for me till one day, while at the gym, I saw this lady. Looking at her I could tell right away that she had some sort of eating disorder, she was skin and bones and working out frantically. I remember going into the steam room and immediately starting to pray for her. I prayed that she would know that she can take up the space that she takes up in the world. I prayed that someone would remind her of the truth of who she is, I prayed that she would know, really know that she was loved, needed and important. Then at that moment I heard a voice say to me, "So why did she show up for you? Where are you trying not to take up the space you take up in the world? Where do you need to be reminded of the truth of who you are? Do you know that you are loved, needed, and important?" It was at that moment that I really got what it means to be connected. When we know that we are connected, we understand that each of us carry something for all of us. I got it. When I heal those things in me that I was praying for in her I give meaning to her suffering. I don't have to and I can't heal her. I just have to clean up my stuff and then, because we are all connected something in her is also healed.

Quote of the day

"Awakening the heart, or the spiritualized mind, is an unlimited process of making the mind more sensitive, focused, energized, subtle and refined, of joining it to its cosmic milieu, the infinity of love."

Kabir Helminski, *Living Presence*

Journal Questions to consider on day 3:

Feel free to use any and as many of these questions as your writing prompt for today.

- What is your connection to your soul and how do you connect?
- What would you like your connection to soul to be?
- What is your collage trying to tell you about your connection to spirit?

Honor what arises in your soul as you set intention for the journey and capture this in your journal.

Activity: Spirit Collage

Things needed:
- Paper
- Magazines
- Colorful Markers, crayons, and/or colored pencils
- Scissors
- Glue
- Tape
- Highlighter
- Stickers (optional)

Find a place where you will not be disturbed. Fold a piece of paper in half. On one half of the paper you are going to make a collage that represents what your current relationship to your soul is and on the other half you will make a collage that represents what you would like your relationship to your soul to be. Give yourself lots of creative freedom. It is amazing what comes up and out when we aren't really thinking but feeling our way through things.

Affirmation of the day

I am one with everything. Everything I am God is. Everywhere I am God is.

FIRE WEEK
We bring the spirit of fire

The eternal flame burns in me
   through the voices of the ancestors guiding my every step
The eternal flame burns in me
   through the passion that pulls me towards that which I love
The eternal flame burns in me
   through the intuition that I carry and the truth that I speak
When my flame burns high you gain sight and understanding
   through the ancestors, through your dreams, and your own instinct

During this week, you will take time to look at what healing is available to you and what messages are present for you in regards to your relationship with the ancestral, dream and spirit worlds. You will connect with your intuition, your creativity and your passion. You will look at your dreams and explore what inspires you. Welcome to the fire.

Fire Posture - Acceptance and Faith

"When I accept the truth of my Earthly existence, both the good and the bad, I can then impact the quality of my living through my Faith in my Divine existence. As a human being, when bad things occur, I will go into denial (This can't be happening to me!) and plunge into despair (There's something wrong with me!). But I can choose to transcend this reactive response and adopt a creative response, by going beyond the limits of my trouble box through asking and thanking my God for revealing the treasure that is always embedded in the challenge."

—Jojopahmaria Nsoroma

 QR code to access Elemental Drumming for Fire Week

Day 4 — Fire Alter

Quote of the Day

*"You are not a human on a spiritual journey.
You are a spirit on a human journey."*

Unknown

Today we start our Fire Week journey. The quote of the day says that we are spiritual beings on a human journey. Standing in this orientation changes everything. When we live from this place, we see everything differently. The things that irritate me don't carry as much weight as we do when we live from the orientation that we are human beings having spiritual experiences. Notice that the quote doesn't ignore the human part of us, it just doesn't lead from that place. We are both human and divine, matter and spirit.

Here we will take a look at our connections, beliefs, attitudes, and practices with the ancestors, the spirit world, and God. Today spend some time thinking about how you wish you were connected to the ancestors, the spirit world, and God.

Journal Questions To Consider On Day 4:

Feel free to use any and as many of these questions as your writing prompt for today.

- When you think about your ancestors, what thoughts and feelings come up for you?
- Do you have any reoccurring dreams, if so what are they?
- Do you want to feel more connected to God and/or the spirit world and in what ways?
- What fear do you have about connecting with your ancestors, God, or the spirit world?
- How do you connect with your own intuition?

Activity: Creating Your Fire Altar

Things needed:
- A space to set up items where they will be undisturbed for the week.
- Items that represent your ancestors, family, and/or your connection to the spirit world.
- A candle or something red to represent fire and the ancestors.

Think about your past and gather items that represent your ancestors, family, and/or connection to God and the spirit world. These items can include but are not limited to photos, jewelry, stones, and a piece of cloth or clothing, anything that brings up memories of ancestors, family, and/or the spirit world. As you gather these items, notice what kinds of things you choose and why. Notice when a thought occurs to include something and you choose not to and then explore why. While doing this, keep in mind that this is your week to focus on the element of fire and the healing that it has for you. Place a candle and/or something red to represent the element of fire. Be very purposeful in choosing your items. It can be as many or as few as you wish.

After gathering all of your items, you need to find a place where you can arrange them in a sacred manner. This place should be a space where the items can stay for the remainder of the week. It should also be a place where you can come back to be with, look at and meditate on these items that you have chosen as you continue this week's fire journey.

Affirmation of the Day

The spirit of my ancestors live in and through me.

Day 5

Quote of the Day

"Every man is a quotation from all his ancestors."

—Ralph Waldo Emerson

Today we will turn to our elders. Our elders hold wisdom that can help support us on our journey. They have had experiences that have provided the opportunity to grow in wisdom and because we are all connected we can learn from their journey. In our culture, so many of us are walking around as adolescent adults. The problem with that is that if we don't have initiated adults, we can't have initiated elders, and if we don't have initiated elders we can't initiate the youth and the cycle of adolescent adulthood continues. Our elders may or may not be related to us. They are the people that we see as the wisdom keepers in our lives. Keep in mind when seeking out your elders that simply being old doesn't make someone an elder; remember an elder carries wisdom. An elder thinks in terms of what serves the larger community. An elder can help to initiate you into who you were meant to be.

Journal Questions To Consider On Day 5:

Feel free to use any and as many of these questions as your writing prompt for today.

- What is an elder?
- Who are my community elders? Who is not?
- How do I connect with my elders?
- How do I learn from them?
- What do I need from my elders that I don't feel I am getting now and how would I be different if I had it?

Activity: Interview an Elder

Things needed:
- Some type of recording device, pencil and paper, audio recorder, video recorder.

Find someone that you see as an elder—someone you see as a wisdom carrier, someone you see as wise. Contact this person and set up a time to interview them. This can be done in person or over the phone or online video call. Some possible interview questions:

- What was it like when you were younger?
- What did you learn from your childhood and why did that matter? What do you value most and why?
- Who are/were the elders in your life?
- What if anything do you do to connect with your own soul and spirit?
- What advice or words of wisdom would you give to those on the path of growing up?
- What advice or words of wisdom do you have for me?
- What do you need in your life to sustain yourself?
- What have been the important lessons of your life?
- Where have you found life's joy?

Feel free to use some or all of these questions and to add some of your own.

Affirmation of the Day

I am an integral part of my story, I am creating a new story today.

Day 6

Quote of The Day

"I maybe here for a short while, gone tomorrow into oblivion or until the days come to take me away. But, in whatever part you play, be remembered as part of a legacy...of sharing dreams and changing humanity for the better, It's that legacy that never dies."

—Unknown

"Then I remember, surprised that I could have ever not, that I am a part of everything and everything is a part of me. Our identities are inseparable."

—Baxter Trautman

Journal Questions to Consider on Day 6:

Feel free to use any and as many of these questions as your writing prompt for today.

- How far back do you know the names of your grandparents?
- What part of the country did your family come from?
- What are some of the traditions you have been given through your family?
- What traditions have you created or adopted for yourself?
- Looking back at your family's history, what behavior patterns can you see?
- What behaviors do you see in yourself that no longer serve you?
- How do you think that same behavior may have been beneficial to your ancestors or to you in the past?

Activity: Getting to Know Your Family Tree

Today, you will look at your family tree and take some time to explore what was happening during the time in history when your ancestors were born. You are invited to place yourself in the story of your ancestral lineage. There are wounds here for many due to traumatic stories of family separation and rupture. The history of slavery in this nation tore Black, Brown and White families apart, leaving gaps in family history and lineage. One of the myths of slavery is that White families stayed intact but we know that isn't true which is evident in this time of ancestry.com when cousins from Black, Brown, a White families are reconnected on a daily basis. For those adopted and raised by those outside of biological family, there can wounds in turning to the family tree, too. We invite the questions and the gaps and the honoring of these as important parts of ourselves.

Fill in the family tree below with the information you know about your family tree (the names of your parents, grandparents, great-grandparents, and your great-great-grandparents). Then next to their names put the year they were born and the year they died; if you aren't sure you can estimate the dates. Now, honor the gaps, questions, and unknown ancestors in your lineage. Create space holders to highlight these ancestors.

This creation—holding both what you know about your ancestral lineage and what you don't know—offers you something to work with when you look back on your lineage and the historical contexts that shaped the lives of your ancestors. What were the collective beliefs during that time in history? What beliefs were formed in reaction to what was happening? What are the collective beliefs that we have picked up along the way? Do those beliefs still serve you or are they old and worn out? Today we get to look at those collective beliefs not only from our families but from our communities as well. Our communities include our families, neighborhoods, our churches, our cities, states, country, and of course our global community. There are clues in these shared stories.

Affirmation of The Day

I open to receive the love and protection the ancestors have for me; they are standing by cheering me on, and watching guard.

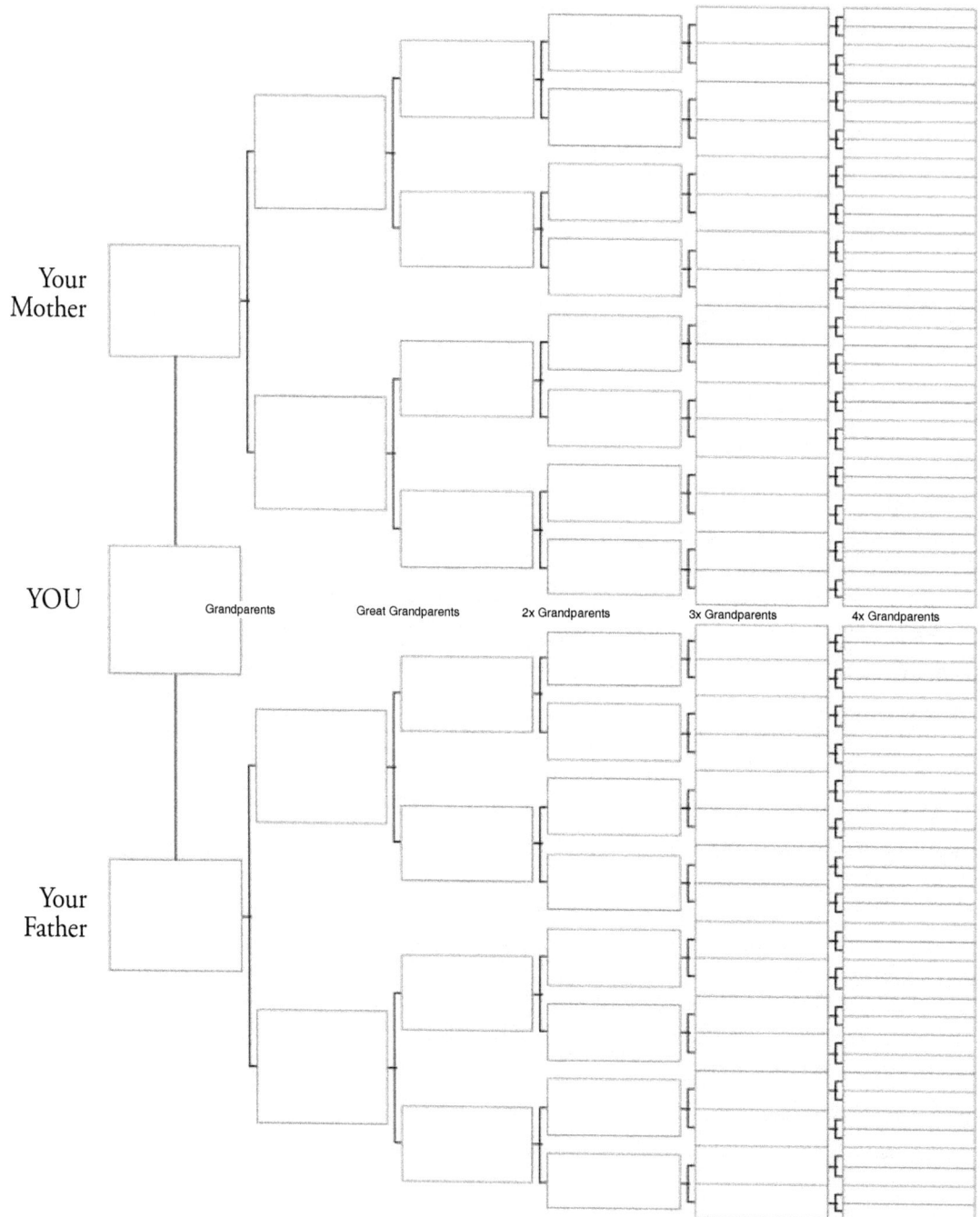

Day 7

Quote of The Day

"Science without religion is lame. Religion without science is blind."
—Albert Einstein

Journal Questions to Consider on Day 7:

Feel free to use any and as many of these questions as your writing prompt for today.

- What are some of the gifts and wounds you received from your ancestors?
- How has systemic racism and White Supremacy affected you and your family?

Note: For White-bodied people, considering in what ways you and your family have been directly impacted by White Supremacy might feel different. Turn the gaze inward and keep it there.

Activity: Messages to the Ancestors

Things needed:
- Biodegradable helium balloons
- Markers

Find a place that has special meaning to you and/or your family. You can go alone or with someone else. Think about your family members or loved ones who have died. Is there things you wish you would have said to them or things you would like to say to them now? Write those things on the balloons with the markers and release the balloons into the sky sending them up to the spirits of your loved ones.

Alternative: visualize this activity. Take time to write down the messages to your ancestors and then imagine sending this off with love.

When my mother-in-law died we, my husband and children would do this activity on what we called her angel birthday, the day she died. We would go to the golf course behind our house and share what we had written and release the balloons into the air. It is always quite an emotional experience. The children now ask for this ritual at other times during the year when they feel the need to connect, on Mother's Day, during the holiday, or just when they want to share some special news with her.

Affirmation of The Day

My traditions and daily practices support my connection to God and the spirit world. The ancestors are cheering me on and standing guard.

Day 8

Quote of The Day

"The spiritual path - is simply the journey of living our lives. Everyone is on a spiritual path; most people just don't know it."

—Marianne Williamson

Journal Questions to consider on day 8:

Feel free to use any and as many of these questions as your writing prompt for today.

- What do you wish for?
- When I was a child I use to pretend...
- A recurring dream that I have is...

Activity: Dreams and Wishes

Things needed:
- Flying Wish Paper or plain paper
- Something to write with
- Matches/lighter
- A container to burn the paper in

The ancestors, our spirit guides, animal totems, angels, and God can't help us if we don't ask because we have been given free will. When we know what we want they can all go to work on our behalf. We so often want God to do our job and we want to do his/hers. We want God to figure out what it is that we want and we want to figure out how to make it happen. Our job is to get as clear as we can on what we want and to surrender the how, when, where, and who. So, spend some time thinking about what it is that you want. I mean what you really want. Get as clear as you can and write it down on a piece of the wish paper, burn it, and watch the smoke carry it up to your spiritual helpers.

Affirmation of The Day
The world is out to gift me and not to get me.

Day 9

Quote of The Day
*"When someone doesn't know their own truth,
yours can often look like ego to them."*
—Quanita

Journal Questions to consider on day 9:
Feel free to use any and as many of these questions as your writing prompt for today.

- What secrets are you holding?
- How long have you been keeping these secrets?
- What are you afraid will happen if you share your secrets?
- How do you think you would feel if you were no longer carrying your secrets?

Activity: Truth Telling
Things needed:
- Someone you trust

Share a secret. I once heard Chris Rock say "Secrets rot the soul." I believe this to be true. As a people, and especially as people of color, we have gotten so good at carrying secrets because there was a time when our lives depended on it. It is how we stayed alive. But a strength over done becomes a weakness. Keeping secrets no longer serves us; as a matter of fact, it is killing us. We have gotten trapped in a prison of our own secrets. It keeps us small. We will never be completely free as long as we are carrying secrets. Secrets often are attached to a sense of shame, blame and/or guilt. We try to keep whatever we find hard to look at in the dark and this gives it power. By shedding light on a secret, it no longer has a hold over us. Find someone who you trust and tell them that you have something that you have been keeping a secret and you would like to share it with them in confidence. Tell them that you don't need them to do anything in response you just want them to listen.

Find a way to release something that you've kept hidden—write it and burn it; share it with a trusted friend; say a prayer of forgiveness and mercy; honor it and hold it with compassion. Make room for your Eternal Flame of Love to shine even brighter.

Affirmation of The Day

I am not my secrets, I am light and love.

Day 10 — Fire Ritual

Quote of The Day
"The inner fire is the most important thing mankind possess."
—Edith Sodergran

Journal Questions to Consider on Day 10:
Feel free to use any and as many of these questions as your writing prompt for today.

- What needs to be released in my life?
- How did what wants to be released serve me in the past?
- What do I want more of in life?
- Ancestors please help me with_____.

Activity: Fire Ritual
Things needed:
- A fire pit/candle
- Lighter
- Pencil or pen
- Paper
- String

Take a walk outside and gather items that you find in nature that represent things that you are ready to let go of in your life. One example may be dead or dying leaves to represent all that needs to die or be let go of or a stick that represents the places in your life where you are too rigid and/or inflexible. Whatever you weren't able to find a representation for but are ready to let go of write it on the paper. Create a bundle, an offering out of these items, say a prayer and offer it to the fire. Thank those things that you are letting go for serving you well and say goodbye to them and put them in the fire. Watch how it burns. Sometimes the fire takes it really fast but sometimes it consumes it slowly. This will give you some information about your letting go of it. Now speak what you want to take the place of what you have just let go of because the universe hates a void and if we don't make clear what we want to fill the place that was just emptied, it will return.

Affirmation of The Day
I release what no longer serves me and open to receiving that which does.

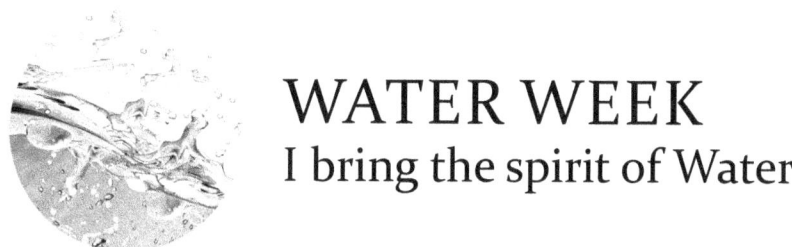

WATER WEEK
I bring the spirit of Water

The Troubled Waters live in me as I bridge communities together

The Troubled Waters live in me through the emotions that float to the surface
The Troubled Waters live in me as I channel grace for forgiveness and reconciliation
My Water heals and transforms with a gentle flow

During this week you will take time to look at what needs to be forgiven and/or reconciled in your life. That can include reconciling things within yourself, your relationships with others, and reconciling old worn out beliefs.

GIFTS OF THE WEEK

Water Posture - Trust & Unconditional Love

"Trust can be easily broken, but it can be repaired, because the ability to trust resides within and is not dependent upon the actions of someone else. And, people can grow and heal from their pain and fear, which is the belief of unconditional love. The lack of trust in a relationship fuels the need for external control (Men/women/teens can't be trusted!) and attachment (I need to figure out how to get that person to do and be what I need in order to trust). Once someone demonstrates that they are untrustworthy a boundary must be set, but we can't make someone change. What we can do through the grace of Forgiveness and unconditional love is to release our attachment to the victim role we played, and accept the person as an evolutionary teacher, come to reveal our pain so we can heal it."

—Jojopahmaria Nsoroma

 QR code to access Elemental Drumming for Water Week

Day 11 — Water Altar

Quote of The Day

"Forgiveness is not saying the offense never happened. It did. Forgiveness is not saying that everything is okay. It isn't. Forgiveness is not saying we no longer feel the pain. We do. I still feel pain, but I am willing to let go of your involvement in my pain. Forgiveness is an attitude of faith whereby you are able to turn over to God the business of how the other party is doing. Forgiveness is saying, "I'm okay, and I am willing to let God deal with whether you are okay, and I am willing to let go of my need to be the instrument of correction and rebuke in your life."

—Len Sweet

Journal Questions to Consider on Day 11:

Feel free to use any and as many of these questions as your writing prompt for today.

- What in your life is asking for reconciliation?
- What things done or left undone need forgiveness?
- What old wounds need tending, now?
- What is your vision of yourself, freed by the gifts of this healing, reconciliation, and forgiveness?

Activity: Creating Your Water Altar

Things needed:
- A space to set up items where they will be undisturbed for the week.
- Items that represent your emotions and what needs to be forgiven or reconciled in your life.
- A candle, something blue and/or water to represent the element of water.

Think about the people and situations in your life that you need to forgive and/or reconcile. Think about the parts of yourself from which you have turned away because you have deemed them ugly or unworthy. Select items that represent these parts of yourself, these people, and situations. These items can include but are not limited to photos, jewelry, stones, pieces of cloth or clothing, anything that connects you to the memory of what needs to be forgiven and/or reconciled.

After gathering all of your items you need to find a place where you can arrange your items in a sacred manner. This place should be a space where items can stay for the remainder of the week. It should also be a place where you can come back to be with, look at and meditate on these items that you have chosen as you continue this week's water journey.

Affirmation of The Day

I (state your name) lovingly forgive myself for all mistakes I have made consciously and unconsciously, known and unknown. I also forgive and release everyone I perceive to have injured or harmed me in any way.

Day 12

Quote of The Day
"Forgiveness is the key to action and freedom."
—Anonymous

Journal Questions to Consider for Day 12:
Feel free to use any and as many of these questions as your writing prompt for today.

- How do I honor my ancestors, angels, spirit guides, and animal spirits?
- What are my animal spirits and how can they help support me?

Activity: Libations
Things needed:
- A special cup, glass, or container
- Water
- A plant or tree to pour libations on

Pouring libations has been a tradition in various countries throughout the continent of Africa. It is a way to honor the ancestors, spirit guides, and animal spirits. This tradition has been carried over from Africa to the United States, through families and in some places through our young people. I have driven down the street and seen on a corner or the side of the road an altar set up where there was a car accident or shooting. On this altar I have noticed bottles. Those bottles are a version of pouring libations. When they are spilling liquid for their homies, they are honoring the ancestors and practicing an old African custom—conscious or not. You can do this alone or with a group. Take your container of water to the plant or tree you have chosen. Speak your gratitude for the ancestor and guides and who they have been to you, then call out the names of the ancestors. This is called an invocation (action of invoking something or someone for assistance), one by one each time pouring a little of the water onto the soil of your plant or tree. Thank them for their guidance, support, and assistance in your life.

Affirmation of The Day

*My ancestors, spirit guides, and animal spirits support my every move.
They are always with me. I am never alone.*

Day 13

Quote of The Day

"The wailing of broken hearts is the doorway to God."

—Rumi

Journal Questions to Consider for Day 13:

Feel free to use any and as many of these questions as your writing prompt for today.

- What pain do you need to let go of?
- What still needs to be grieved in your life?
- When and where in your life did you learn that it wasn't okay to grieve?

Activity: Wailing

Things needed:
- A quiet, secluded safe space
- Someone to hold sacred space for you (this can and will include the ancestors)

Wailing

Definition:
- to utter a prolonged, inarticulate, mournful cry, usually high-pitched or clear-sounding, as in grief or suffering
- to make mournful sounds, as music or the wind.
- to lament or mourn bitterly
- howl, bawl, yowl, cry, moan, groan; shriek, scream, holler, yelp.

Grief is essential to love, praise, compassion, and joy. Without grief there is no life or living. For anything to grow there is the need for water. It took me a long time to realize that grief isn't suffering, it doesn't even have to include suffering. One of the biggest lies we tell ourselves about grief is that we all grieve differently. I don't believe this to be true, I believe we all avoid grief differently. We avoid grief through numbing out by over working, keeping busy, drinking, getting lost in media, using drugs, overeating and having sex. Grieving is the same for each of us because grief is just the release of the emotions that are inside. Without the ability to grieve our compassion is very shallow. Being willing to go deep into our own grief gives our compassion depth because we can't give what we don't have.

Go to the place you have chosen for this activity and call in the ancestors you poured libations for yesterday. Ask that they hold the space for you while you do your grieving. If you have invited other people to participate in this ritual with you, you can hold the space for each other and the ancestors can also support you in holding the circle. Share what you need to grieve with your support. Share how this pain has affected you and how you feel it has blocked you. Allow yourself to feel the pain and to use sound and tones to let it out of your body. There are different sounds of grief. When we tap into these sounds we can release something deep down that we couldn't reach with mere words. So today, spend some time with your grief. Surrender to it completely for a bit. Letting it flow through you is how we are able to make it to the gifts that wait for us on the other side of our grief. When you feel complete thank the ancestors and the people supporting you for their service.

Affirmation of the day

My wailing touches and releases my grief and make room for my joy.

Day 14

Quote of the day

"You didn't come into this world. You came out of it, like a wave from the ocean. You are not a stranger here."

—Alan Watts

Journal Questions to consider for day 14:

Feel free to use any and as many of these questions as your writing prompt for today.

- What are the different roles you play in your life?
- What have been significant moments in your life?
- What have been important signals at turning-points in your life?
- What are you seeking?

Activity: Quilting

Things needed:
- Pieces of fabric
- Needle + thread (or fabric glue)
- Alternative: paper/magazines/glue

African symbols were hidden in African American quilts to help communicate messages. It was a secret communication system. Slaves weren't allowed to read and write so quilts were a perfect way to communicate. Quilts allow for messages that could be hidden and in plain sight all at the same time. In the book *Hidden in Plain View: A Secret Story of Quilts and the Underground Railroad* the authors, Jacqueline L. Tobin and Raymond G. Dobard, Ph.D. write:

"African secret society signs and symbols are still hidden in decorative textile designs. Examples include Bogolanfini cloth painted by Bamana women in Mali; Adinkra cloth stamped by Ashanti men in Ghana; Adire cloth painted by Yoruba women with designs said to have been given to them by Oshun, the goddess of wealth and fertility in Nigeria; Epke (Leopard) society cloth resist-dyed by Ejagham women with nsibidi secret society signs in Nigeria; and Kuba cloth woven with

designs which allude to the central African Kongo cosmogram, a diamond or a cross which represents the four moments of the sun or the soul: birth, life, death, and rebirth in the watery ancestral realm."

As I learn more about quilting and what meaning it has for descendants of slaves, I am struck by how the piecing together of what may have been seen as useless scraps helped to point the way to freedom. The symbols—along with some forms of dance, songs, words, and phrases—allowed them to communicate about the Underground Railroad without slave owners' knowledge.

You can do this activity a couple of ways. You can gather pieces of fabric you have from items that are important to you and sew them together with a simple stitch or buy some fabric glue to connect your pieces. You can quilt a square in a pattern used during slavery to communicate a message, or you can make your own design that represents something from your own personal journey.

Monkey Wrench
This tells about tools you might need for the journey.

Crossroads
The crossroads was in Cleveland, Ohio. This was the last stop on the Underground Railroad before crossing over to Canada.

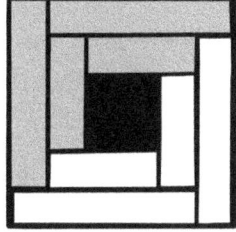
Log Cabin
You have reached a safe house.

Bow Ties
This is a message that you will need to disguise yourself and someone will bring you clothes.

Flying Geese
Follow the geese north to freedom.

Drunkard's Path
Slave hunters are close, go back to avoid them.

North Star
The North Star will help you navigate your way north towards Canada.

Tumbling Blocks
It's time to pack up, it will be soon time to go

Affirmation of the day

I was birthed from community with exactly what the world needs with all the right pieces.

Day 15

Quote of the day
"Be water my friend."
—Bruce Lee

Journal Questions to Consider for Day 15:

Feel free to use any and as many of these questions as your writing prompt for today.

- Who do you still need to forgive and for what do they need to be forgiven?
- Who do you need to ask forgiveness from and for what?

Activity: Forgiveness Letters

Things needed:
- Pencil
- Paper

Okay, if you are anything like me, the thought of writing forgiveness letters sends fear through your body. First, let us put your mind at ease, this exercise doesn't include mailing the letters, just writing them. There is power in just being expressed through writing. There is power in giving voice to what has been unspoken.

Think of someone or someones that you need to forgive or someone you need forgiveness from (one of the letters may be to yourself). Sit and write them a letter. Be sure to include what you are forgiving or what you are asking forgiveness for in the letter. Also include how you feel and what you would like to see happen.

Affirmation of the day

I flow through my day like water with ease and grace

Day 16

Quote of the day

*"Communication leads to community, that is,
to understanding, intimacy and mutual valuing."*

—Rollo May

Journal Questions to Consider for Day 16:

Feel free to use any and as many of these questions as your writing prompt for today.

- What are the things in your life that you have dreamed of but have seemed impossible?
- What reasons did you have for not pursuing those dreams?
- What beliefs do you hold that support your reasons for not pursuing those dreams?

Activity: "I can't" funeral

Things needed:
- Paper
- Something to write with

"Friends, we gather today to honor the memory of *I Can't*. While he was with us on earth, he touched the lives of everyone, some more than others. His names, unfortunately, have been spoken in every public building - schools, city halls, and state capitols and yes, even The White House.

We have provided *I Can't* with a final resting place and headstone that contains his epitaph. He is survived by his brothers and sisters, *I can; I will'; I'm going to Right Away.'* They are not as well known as their famous relative and are certainly not as strong and powerful yet. Perhaps someday, with your help, they will make an even bigger mark on the world. May *I Can't* rest in peace and may everyone present pick up their lives and move forward in his absence. Amen."

Affirmation
I am. I can. I will.

Day 17 — Water Ritual

Quote of the day

"Water is powerful. It can wash away earth, put out fire, and even destroy iron. Water can carve it's way through stone. And when trapped, water makes a new path."

—Arthur Golden

Questions to Consider for Day 17:

Feel free to use any and as many of these questions as your writing prompt for today.

- What are you ready to let go of?
- What aren't you ready to let go of?
- What still needs to be forgiven?

Activity:
Things needed:
- Container
- Water
- An offering/gift

Get a container of water. It can be a water bottle or a special container you have for carrying water, and fill it with water. I collect rain water during the year to have water for my rituals but that's not necessary. You can use whatever water you have available. Take this container to a body of water: pond, lake, river, or ocean. You might also want to take an offering to the water. This could include flowers, tobacco, a stone or an object that has been imbued with your love. Say a prayer, place the offering into the water if you have one; speak into the container of water what it is that you would like the water to help you release, then pour the water from the container into the pond, lake, river, or ocean.

Affirmation of the day
I am complete and perfect in every way, lacking no essential quality.

EARTH WEEK
I bring the spirit of the earth

*Mother Earth lives in me, in my walk, in my stance,
   in the holding of my deep roots
Mother Earth lives in me in the foundation that she provides
   through me for so many people
Mother Earth lives in me in my ability to create and give birth
   to the new
When I shift the earth quakes*

During this week you will take time to examine where we come from and to whom we belong through the element of earth. Earth can invite us into nurture and care and support us in shifting from our orientation from one of scarcity to one of abundance.

GIFTS OF THE WEEK

Earth Posture - Personal Sovereignty & Vulnerability

"We must be grounded in the truth of who we are — Divine beings on a mission to choose love over fear — in order to have relationships that are authentic, loving and supportive of our truth. Until we are able to believe that people can love us for our truth, our insecurity and co-dependency (external focus on what someone thinks of me and no internal consideration of what I think of my Self), are evidence of an undeveloped belief in our supreme and independent power/authority over and responsibility for our thoughts, choices, and resulting behaviors. Authenticity emerges from vulnerability which comes from a willingness to feel and to experience not knowing."

—Jojopahmaria Nsoroma

 QR code to access Elemental Drumming for Earth Week

"The earth is our origin and destination. The ancient rhythms of the earth have insinuated themselves into the rhythms of the human heart. The earth is not outside us; it is within: the clay from where the tree of the body grows. When we emerge from our offices, rooms and houses, we enter our natural element. We are children of the earth: people to whom the outdoors is home. Nothing can separate us from the vigour and vibrancy of this inheritance. In contrast to our frenetic, saturated lives, the earth offers a calming stillness."
—John O'Donohue

Day 18 — Earth Alter

Quote of the day

"Everyone has talent. What is rare is the courage to nurture it in solitude and to follow the talent to the dark places where it leads."

—unknown

Journal Questions to Consider for Day 18:

Feel free to use any and as many of these questions as your writing prompt for today.

- What helps you to feel grounded?
- Where in your life do you want to invite in more abundance and why?
- What nurture and care do you need to allow yourself to have?

Activity: Creating Your Earth Altar

Things needed:
- Sacred place for altar
- Items to place on altar

Think about where you most feel at home. What items represent home, family, your roots, nurturing, abundance and care. Add items that are made of the earth like pottery, or clay figures. Add things that are the color of the earth element, yellow, beige, and brown, this can include flowers and fruit. Most of all listen deeply to what connects you to the earth.

After gathering all of your items you need to find a place where you can arrange your items in a sacred manner. This place should be a space where items can stay for the remainder of the week. It should also be a place where you can come back to be with, look at and meditate on these items that you have chosen as you continue this week's earth journey.

Affirmation of the day

I am at home with myself.

Day 19

Quote of the day

"A people without the knowledge of their past history, origin and culture is like a tree without roots"

—Marcus Garvey

Journal Questions to Consider on Day 19:

Feel free to use any and as many of these questions as your writing prompt for today.

- What nourishes your mind, body, spirit?
- What does this nourishment feel like?
- How might you nourish your whole self in new ways?

Activity: Soul Food

Things Needed:
- Recipe
- Ingredients
- Ancestor plate

Pick an ancestral dish to cook—some food dish that has been passed down through your family. It can be a dish that you have made before or you could contact a family member for a recipe that you have wanted to learn. Be aware that you might get a recipe that includes "add a little pinch of this or that to taste", because this is a part of our history. During slavery most slaves weren't allowed to learn how to read and write so they didn't have written recipes, every time they cooked they were said to have to cooked from the soul. This is where the term "soul food" came from. Whatever your history, there are foods that are a part of your familial stories.

Gather everything you need to prepare your dish. As you are gathering the ingredients, be mindful of what your ancestors had to do to gather these same items, and consider if they even had access to all the things you are using now. You might go to the store to gather the ingredients; they may have had to grow them. You may turn on the faucet to get your water, they may have had to get their's from a well. Honoring their journey can help us be in gratitude for ours. When the meal is complete, set a plate on the table for the ancestors. Feed them first. Put some of each of the foods you make on the plate and offer thanks to them and then enjoy.

Affirmation of the day
The food I eat brings nourishment to my mind, body, and soul.

Day 20

Quote of the day

"The meaning of life is to find your gift. The purpose of life is to give it away."
—Pablo Picasso

Journal Questions to Consider on Day 20:

Feel free to use any and as many of these questions as your writing prompt for today.

- What makes you come alive? In what ways do you feel Life's force moving through you?
- How might you ground yourself in this life source as you co-create your life?
- How might you offer this aliveness to those around you? To the world?

Activity: Give Away

Things Needed:
- Three items to giveaway

The world often makes it hard for us to know our gifts; we are conditioned to fit into roles and take up on the masks that allow us to "fit in" and "belong". In doing so, we forget who we are, whose we are. Our gifts are not fully realized and lay wasted and forgotten, our world the less for it. Howard Thurman helps us remember our gifts: *"Don't ask what the world needs. Ask what makes you come alive, and go do it. Because what the world needs is people who have come alive."*

This is an activity about generosity and abundance—receiving and giving. We are blessed with so much in our lives, sometimes we need to acknowledge it and make an offering. Find three items that you own that have special meaning for you. Think about the people in your life and who you would like to gift these items to. While identifying the items be sure to use discernment in deciding what items to give away and to who to give them..

Affirmation of the day
Life is so filled with abundance and it flows through me effortlessly.

Day 21

Quote of the day

"A nations culture resides in the hearts and souls of its people."
—Mahatma Gandhi

Journal Questions to Consider on Day 21:

Feel free to use any and as many of these questions as your writing prompt for today.

- What are the things in your life that have most shaped who you are?
- What were your favorite foods growing up?
- What were some of your family traditions?

Activity: I am from...

Things needed:
- Pen
- Paper

Find a quiet place to sit or lay down where you will not be disturbed. Take a couple of minutes to think about your family when you were young. How was growing up for you? Who were the people in your life that you felt closest to? Who were the people you were afraid of? Who if anyone taught you that it was safe to trust yourself? Who loved you in a way that you felt it? What did their love look like? Open your eye and just start writing, starting each line with the prompt, *I am from...*

Here is a group poem done by a group of women who attended my (Quanita's) 2009 Feminine Wisdom Retreat; their prompt was *We come from...*

We Come From

We come from women who rose in the face of adversity, who chose to keep living today in hope of a better tomorrow

We come from an embryo of good intention, coated in fear, pain, and power struggles

We come from women who wanted more for their children then they ever had

We come from the stars

We come from women who were strong, but afraid to show emotion

We come from women who can sit in a circle and laugh until they cry

We come from women who were broken, bitter, and loving still

We come from women who allow their emotions to speak louder than their words

We come from women who learned how to be women from men

We come from generational curses we refuse to pass on

We come from women truth tellers and women who knew how to keep a secret

We come from women who were and still are addicted to the drama

We come from women who were sick and kept trying to help others that could help themselves

We come from trees, cliffs, and rolling hills

We come from women who cook from their souls

We come from grandmothers who licked their fingers when they ate birthday cake

We come from women who sat us on their laps and sang us to sleep

—Written by the women of Nzuzu's 2009 Feminine Wisdom Retreat

Affirmation of The Day
I come from and live in wholeness.

Day 22

Quote of the day
"Self-care is not about self-indulgence, it's about self-preservation."
—Audrey Lorde

Journal Questions to Consider on Day 22:
Feel free to use any and as many of these questions as your writing prompt for today.

- How do I feel about my hair?
- What are the stories that I've heard about hair like mine?
- Have I ever been asked to change my hair because someone else felt it was inappropriate?
- What are you routines for tending to your hair?

Activity: Hair
Things Needed:
- Shampoo
- Water for washing hair

Wash your hair in loving kindness. In some villages throughout the continent of Africa, your hair could communicate a lot about who you were. It could tell if you were married or not, what age you were, if you had children, what tribe you belong to and who your family was.

Affirmation of the day
I love my hair.

Day 23

Quote of the day

*"Nurture your minds with great thoughts.
To believe in the heroic makes heroes."*

—Benjamin Disraeli

Our bodies are the sites for violence, judgement and pain; they are the sites of creation, love, and pleasure. Our bodies join heaven and earth. They are homes where our Spiritual beings incarnate. Consider the skin that holds our beingness; the skin that both contains us and connects us with all else.

Journal Questions to Consider on Day 23:

Feel free to use any and as many of these questions as your writing prompt for today.

- In what ways does our skin evidence our scars and beauty marks?
- What might we learn from our skin's capacity to grow and stretch and return?
- What does the world tell us about our skin? What do we know to be true, as we occupy it and belong to it and unite with it?

Activity: Skin

Things Needed:
- Pen
- Paper

Loving the skin you are in:
Make a list of all the beautiful things that you know that are the same color as the color of your skin. Don't forget to add yourself to your list.

Affirmation of the day

I am grateful for the skin I am in; it holds my body, mind, soul and spirit.

Day 24 — Earth Ritual

Quote of the day

"If we are to have peace on earth, our loyalties must become ecumenical rather than sectional. Our loyalties must transcend our race, our tribe, our class, and our nation; and this means we must develop a world perspective."

—Martin Luther King Jr.

Journal Questions to consider on day 24:

Feel free to use any and as many of these questions as your writing prompt for today.

- In what ways do you feel earth's abundant giving?
- How are you blessed with earth's beauty and life?

Activity: Gifting Throughout The Day

Things Needed:
- Artifacts/items/opportunities that make themselves available for giving.

Gifting throughout your day: Look for moments to make offerings and gifts as you move through your day. These can be small acts or grand ones: anything from listening with care and patience and offering eye contact, to reaching out to an old friend. How might these gifts be creative—perhaps in the form of love note or poem or prayer or song—so that the gift is sourced from you.

Affirmation of the day

I am the source of creativity and abundance. Gifting this creativity is life-affirming.

MINERAL WEEK
I bring the spirit of the minerals

The Ancient Minerals live in me through the stories of those who have gone before
The Ancient Minerals live in me through a knowing that seems to come out of nowhere
The Ancient Minerals live in me through the wisdom that I carry in my bones
My Mineral runs deep and wise and connects the past, present, and future

During this week you will take time to work with our stories and our relationship with energy.

Gifts of the Week

Mineral Posture - Curiosity and Excitement

"As humans, our natural curiosity and ability to learn is what makes life exciting. Before standardized testing, a person was more able to discover and value their genius – like Phyllis Wheatley, Thomas Edison, and my grandfather, who could fix anything in and around the house. None of them took an SAT or an ACT. Arrogance and our addiction to anxiety are the obvious results when the love of learning and discovery of loving purpose is overshadowed by competitive measurements of intelligence to determine quality of life."

—Jojopahmaria Nsoroma

 QR code to access Elemental Drumming for Mineral Week

Day 25 — Mineral Altar

Quote of the day

"Life hangs on a narrative thread. This thread is a braid of stories that inform us about who we are, and where we come from, and where we might go. The thread is slender but strong: we trust it to hold us and allow us to swing over the edge of the known into the future we dream in words."

—Christina Baldwin

Journal Questions to Consider on Day 25:

Feel free to use any and as many of these questions as your writing prompt for today.

- What stories have been passed down that you want to honor and release?
- What stories do you want to create and carry into the future?
- Who have been the wisdom and story-keepers in your life? What forms do these stories take?

Activity: Creating Your Mineral Altar

This week our altar is focused on our stories. You can choose items that are connected to your ancestral stories or to the stories that you carry. This is also connected to communication, so if there are things that you need help communicating, you could put something on the altar that represents that issue as well.

Affirmation of the day

Yesterday's stories + today's wisdom = tomorrow's reality.

Day 26

Quote of the day
"If you cannot get rid of the family skeleton, you may as well make it dance."
—George Bernard Shaw

Journal Questions to Consider on Day 26:
Feel free to use any and as many of these questions as your writing prompt for today.

- What are the things in your life that you feel you have to do?
- Where are you most likely to give up your power of choice?

Activity: Write or Tell Your *Victim* Story
Things Needed:
- Pen
- Paper

Write your victim story. We all have victim stories that allow us to occupy passive roles in our own lives. Expressing these stories outwardly can be a powerful way to acknowledge the truth underneath these stories—that there is always choice and with that choice, comes power.

Affirmation of the day
There is always choice. Remembering this, I can never be a victim.

Day 27

Quote of the day

*"Storytelling is the essential human activity.
The harder the situation the more essential it is."*

—Tim O'Brien

Journal Questions to Consider on Day 27:

Feel free to use any and as many of these questions as your writing prompt for today.

- When have you faced your fears and spoken/acted in your own truth?
- When have you overcome a barrier or obstacle—either internal or external—and acted in courage and perseverance?

Activity: Write or Tell Your *Victor* Story

Things Needed:
- Pen
- Paper

Write your story about victory or find someone to bear witness to your victory story. You can start your story with *once upon a time*...and share how you have been victorious. Note where you have come from and what obstacles you have overcome. Share the dragons you have slayed and the angels along the way.

Until lions tell their tale, the story of the hunt will always glorify the hunter
—African Proverb

Affirmation of the day

I am powerful beyond measure. The story I tell myself is mine to choose.

Day 28

Quote of the day

"We've got this gift of love, but love is like a precious plant.
You can't just accept it and leave it in the cupboard
or just think it's going to get on by itself.
You've got to keep on watering it. You've got to really look after it and nurture it."

—John Lennon

Journal Questions to Consider on Day 28:

- What do you now about nourishing and tending to your energy?
- What gives you energy and what takes away your energy?

Activity: Energy Work

Things Needed:
- Three different locations/environment

Mineral is not only the element of stories but also a conduit of energy. Today we will work with energy. There are lots of ways of knowing; using the yardstick of what is white and male, we tend to prioritize ways of knowing that are connected to the five senses: touch, taste, hear, see, and smell. Today you will bring your attention to how your energy feels when you are in different spaces and with different people. Choose three different environments to practice. Notice your own energy in those places, with those people. What did you learn about what gives you energy and what takes away your energy? As you practice this more and more, it will become easier to feel the spaces you are in; you will be more capable of managing your own energy.

Affirmation of the day

Learning to manage my energy is more important than learning to manage my time.

Day 29

Quote of the day

"Never, no, never did Nature say one thing and Wisdom say another."
—Edmund Burke

Journal Questions to consider on day 29:

Feel free to use any and as many of these questions as your writing prompt for today.

- What was the money story that you grew up with?
- How has that story helped to shape your money story today?
- What is the money story you would like to be living?

Activity: Money Story

Things Needed:
- $10, $20, $50, or $100 dollar bill

Take a bill, it can be a $10, $20, $50, or $100, something that is a stretch but isn't going to break you and put it in your wallet. Make a pledge to yourself not to spend this money. This money is to remind you of your abundance. As you walk through your day and see things that you would like to buy your story can change from *I don't have the money* to *I don't choose to spend my money on this right now.* It moves you from a place of lack to a place of abundance.

Affirmation of the day

There is always more than enough for what needs to be done.

Day 30

Quote of the day
"I am means I am free."
—*Mooji*

Journal Questions to consider on day 30:
Feel free to use any and as many of these questions as your writing prompt for today

- What do our shadows have to teach us?
- What feelings come up for you when you consider your shadows?
- And what it feel like to open to all parts of yourself and accept it all as part of the whole?

Activity: Shadow Work—What aren't you seeing?
Things needed:
- A witness—friend/companion/colleague

We all need witnesses to be seen. Ask someone you trust to help yourself see your whole self: *Can you help me see and honor my whole self by describing aspects of myself you think I'd be surprised to hear? Things you've noticed about me and never shared? Alternate stories about myself then the ones I hold? I'm asking you because I trust you and I want to hear Truth.*

Ask and then receive their insight. Consider how it feels to receive this. Give gratitude—for their witness and to yourself for receiving it. Give gratitude for your shadows too as you draw them closer to your awareness.

Affirmation of the day
I gather all parts of me together in a glorious, messy, humanly-divine whole. I am. And I am grateful.

Day 31 — Mineral Ritual

Quote of the day

"You can't start the next chapter in your life if you keep re-reading the last one."
—Unknown

Journal Questions to consider on day 31:

Feel free to use any and as many of these questions as your writing prompt for today.

- What old stories no longer serve you?
- What new ones do you want to author?

Activity: Two Stones; Two Stories

Things Needed:
- Two stones

Choose two stones: one representing an old story of yourself and one representing the new story of who you are and who you are becoming. Take the "old stone" in your hands. Give gratitude for how the old stories have served you; breathe this gratitude in and feel it in your bones as you hold this stone. Place it in a special place with care (maybe in the soil of a potted plant or outside near a tree: *Thank you, old story for your service. I release you.* Now, take the "new stone" in your hand. Utter your new story into it and give gratitude for its holding this story with care as you live into this story. *Thank you, new story for growing me into who I am becoming and who I am meant to be.* Take this stone and place it with care on your mineral altar.

Affirmation of the day

I am the author of my own story; I choose the story of who I am.

NATURE WEEK
I bring the spirit of Nature

The Playful Nature lives in me through magic that transforms and grows

The Playful Nature lives in me standing at the gates of all Rites of Passage

The Playful Nature lives in me as the trickster spreading joy and laughter

My Nature tosses aside the mask that you wear to unveil the truth of who you really are

During this week you will take time to invite in the magic of nature and its ability to heal and transform.

Gifts of the Week
Nature Posture - Fulfillment & Gratitude

"Fulfillment is the experience of fullness and satisfaction in the heart and soul, and gratitude is the attitude that enables us to live fully. We feel fulfillment and then we act grateful. Then along comes some form of trauma that awakens our pain body which teaches us coping mechanisms for numbing and ignoring the pain. And, when we numb our pain we also numb our ability to feel what is enough. Combine this with satisfaction overshadowed by competition, and the forgetting of the cosmic law that to everything there is a season, we will embrace greediness (The more I have, the better I will be), and envy (The grass is always greener on the other side) as postures for success. Of course we will only succeed at becoming more insatiable and frustrated by a no-win pursuit of happiness."

—Jojopahmaria Nsoroma

 QR code to access Elemental Drumming for Nature Week

Day 32 — Nature Altar

Quote of the day
"Change is inevitable, growth is optional."
—Jojopah Maria Nsoroma

*"Movement and growth in nature takes time.
The patience of nature enjoys the ease of trust and hope."*
—John O'Donohue

Journal Questions to consider on day 32:

Feel free to use any and as many of these questions as your writing prompt for today.

- Where is there movement in your life that you want to elevate to support further change?
- Where is there stagnation that is blocking change?
- Where are there elements of play and wild that catalyze movement?

Activity: Creating Your Nature Altar

Things Needed:
- Special place
- Items/artifacts to place on your altar

This week our altar is centered on change and transformation. Consider the questions above and gather artifacts to include on your altar that inspires the change that you are seeking and/or the change that is already underway in your life.

Affirmation of the day:

Life's flow is deep, fun, and easy.

Day 33

Quote of the day

"Showing gratitude is one of the simplest yet the most powerful things humans can do for each other."

—Randy Pausch

Journal Questions to consider on day 33:

Feel free to use any and as many of these questions as your writing prompt for today.

- What might I reclaim in my life that is both the key to my liberation and the key that is imprisoning me?
- What beats return me home to myself, to Spirit?
- How might I practice these beats so that I am come alive?

Activity: Drumming

The Akan Drum is a drum that is believed to be the oldest surviving African American artifact to exist. The drum was made in the Ghana region of West Africa somewhere between 1700 and 1775 and is believed to have traveled on a slave ship to America. Because slaves left with nothing, it is believed to have been brought on the slave ship by a member of the crew. The drum was used to "dance the slaves" as a form of exercise to keep them strong during the journey. It currently resides in the British Museum. This drum holds some information for us about the different ways of being. This drum shows us an early example of the clash of cultures. It shows the drum being used as a tool for exercise by a Eurocentric crew but in African culture the drum was used for connection to soul and spirit, and as transportation to another time, state, and space. Sobonfu Somé, of Burkina Faso said, "The beat of the drum is the tuning of the soul. Think about this for a minute: the drum—the very thing that was used as a tool for liberation—was taken and used as a tool of oppression. The good news is that each one of us can use this conduction tool to help us reclaim our own freedom.

Find a drum or something to drum on and a place where you can connect with your own soul through the drum. Spend a couple of minutes just listening and feeling into yourself and your surroundings. Then when you can hear a beat in your head calling you start playing your drum. Continue to listen and to play. Pay attention to how you feel. Notice if the beat is fast or slow, deep and soulful, or light and playful. What does the beat have to teach you? Where is the beat trying to take you? When you feel complete return to you journal and write some of your experience down.

Affirmation of the day

The beat of the drum is the tuning of the soul. No one can take away my drumbeat.

Day 34

Quote of the day

"All I know for certain is that this is how I want to spend my life - collaborating to the best of my ability with forces of inspiration that I can neither see, nor prove, nor command, nor understand."

—Elizabeth Gilbert

Journal Questions to Consider on Day 34:

Feel free to use any and as many of these questions as your writing prompt for today.

- What are some of the masks you wear and why?
- When did you first start wearing this mask and what was happening in your life?

The Mask

Laugh, they said
as I reached for the mask that
shows them who they want to see.

Smile, they said
as my hands slipped into the
pockets of protection
unseen.

Quiet, they said
as the wind in my voice
pushed against
the cover over my
weary heart.

Behind the wounds,

(still
anchored in the dirt and rock,
showered by the trees,
kissed by rainbows and stars,
cradled by the wings of Hawk,)

I am here;

clutching this mask
in hopes of
learning to
navigate

an untamed world

knowing that
one day I may rip it off

and they will
see that it was me

all along.

—Timi Singley

Activity Mask Making

Things Needed:
- Paper mache mask or a form of a mask
- Art supplies to decorate (paint, glue, beads, feathers, magazines)

Ritual and ceremonial mask have been used throughout different cultures and on the continent of Africa to communicate with the ancestral world, connect with animal spirits, celebrate special occasions, and honor community members. This mask can also represent a characteristic that you want to bring more into your life, as in courage, beauty, strength, compassion, masculinity, or femininity.

Affirmation of the day

The mask I wear and show the outside world reflects my inner truth.

Day 35

Quote of the day

"She's mad but she's magic. There's no lie in her fire."
—Charles Bukowski

Journal Questions to Consider on Day 35:

Feel free to use any and as many of these questions as your writing prompt for today.

- Why are you worthy of love?
- What do you love and cherish about your self?
- What unique gifts live within you?

Activity Love Letter to Self

Things Needed:
- Paper
- Pen, pencil, or some other object for writing

Write a love letter to yourself. Sit down and think about all the things you love about you. If you have trouble starting, ask someone who loves you to share with you what they love about you: this should get the ball rolling. Remember this is a love letter and not a I kind of like you sort of letter. Think of the times you have made it through, think of the gratitude you have for tough decisions you have had to make, put it all in there. What do you think your best features are? What do you do well? Put it in there! Also spend some time on expressing your love for yourself just because; not because you have earned it but because you just love you.

Affirmation of the day

*I love you*_____ *(Your Name).*

_____
_____
_____

Day 36

Quote of the day
"Growth and comfort do not coexist."
—Ginni Rometty

Journal Questions to consider on day 36:

Feel free to use any and as many of these questions as your writing prompt for today.

- Name an animal that you were drawn to as a child.
- What about this animal do you love or is attractive to you?
- Name an animal you you are afraid of as a child.
- What about this animal scares you?
- Is there an animal to means a lot to you now? Why?

Activity - Animal Wisdom

Things Needed:
- Pen or pencil
- Paper

Today your task is to notice the animals that you see throughout the day. These can be real live animals, animal figurines, stuffed animals, animals on a show that you are watching, animals in your dreams, and/or animals in magazines. It all counts. Make a list and alongside your list write a couple of characteristics for each animal. Look at your list of characteristics. What does this list have to do with who you are and who you are becoming?

Affirmation of the day

Every animal has a story to tell and a gift to give.

Day 37

Quote of the day
"Growth is the only evidence of life."
—John Henry Newman

"Movement and growth in nature takes time.
The patience of nature enjoys the ease of trust and hope.
There is something in our clay nature that needs to continually experience this ancient, outer ease of the world.
It helps us remember who we are and why we are here."
—John O'Donohue, *Beauty: The Invisible Embrace*

Journal Questions to Consider on Day 37
- In what ways do we separate ourselves from nature?
- Where do we experience connection with nature?
- How does that connection bring life?

Activity: Connect with Nature
Things Needed:
- Self
- Space to enjoy and be in/with nature=
- An offering to give in thanks to nature.

It is easy to think of nature as external to us. We are nature and are in relationship with the natural world. This activity invites reconnecting with the nature within us, a remembering of ourselves in relationship with all the universe. Devote some time to be in a natural setting, in your backyard or a nearby park; perhaps it is even in your home, near a plant or window. First, gather a gift to offer—tobacco, sweetgrass, cedar, sage, or a prayer; keep a half of this offering for the next day's ritual and take a half on your time with nature. As you begin the time with nature, open your whole self to all that surrounds you. Notice the smells, the sounds, the taste and welcome all. Notice how often you look for beauty and release that "taking" energy and the expectations that follow it. Allow nature to show up just as it is; being in authentic relationship is to move out of the position of "taker" and into mutuality. Listen and be attentive for what comes—animal spirits, wind, sounds. Simply be with nature in this place and sense it opening in you, your own internal sense of spaciousness. When it is time, offer your gift of gratitude.

Affirmation of the day:

I am nature; I am re-membering my place in the web of life.

Day 38 — Nature Ritual

Quote of the day

"Look deep into nature and then you will understand everything better."
—Albert Einstein

Journal Questions to Consider on Day 38—Nature Ritual

Feel free to use any and as many of these questions as your writing prompt for today.

- In what ways is nature alive in me?
- In what ways do I experience myself as in relationship with Nature?

Activity: Nature Ritual

Things Needed:
- Remains of the offering from yesterday

Gather the remaining of the gift you offered yesterday in gratitude for nature. Sit in front of your Nature Altar and reflect on your experience with nature yesterday. Notice what arises in your body as you remember. Feel your own natural being and your inherent interconnectedness with the natural world. Place this offering on the altar, honoring life's interconnectedness and how you play an essential role in the web of life.

Affirmation of the day

I am in alignment with the natural world; I am just right where I am and who I am,

DAY 39 — INTEGRATION

Quote of the day

"Internal integration can bring a person back from the grave."
—Quanita Roberson

Journal Questions to consider on day 39 — Integration

Feel free to use any and as many of these questions as your writing prompt for today.

- What are the parts of myself that I am welcoming back home?
- What have I discovered about who I am?
- Where have I experienced healing throughout this journey?
- Can I see how my intentions from the beginning (body, mind, & soul) have shown up in this journey and if so how?

Activity

Things Needed:
- Pen or pencil
- Paper

I used to be, but now I am.

Find a piece of paper and fill in the following statement.
I used to be _____ but now I am _____.
You can write as many as you are called to write but try to find at least three.

Affirmation of the day

I am.

Day 40 — Return & Intention Setting

Quote of the day

"Every ending is creating the space and opening for an amazing new beginning."
—Bryant McGill

Journal Questions to consider on day 40

One last question:
What are my hopes and dreams moving forward?

Activity: Set Intentions

- Pen or pencil
- Journal/notebook

Time to set new intentions for your body, mind, and spirit. You can do this by writing in your journal or by starting the 40 day journey again.

Affirmation of the day:

My InnerGround Railroad to soul and spirit is always available and offers deepening freedom, love, and forgiveness.

THE AUTHORS

QUANITA ROBERSON

I am the promise of forgiveness and reconciliation in the world. I haven't always known this but I have always been moving toward it. I started my healing journey at a young age. I am a shaman. It has taken me a long time to grow into this...to grow into me. Mostly because I never quite understood why a person would choose this life. Now I understand that it chooses you.

I believe we are in a time that is calling us to remember. Remember what really matters. Remember the truth of who we really are. Remember that we belong to each other.

I am a facilitator dedicated to addressing embedded trauma. I am a spiritual teacher, speaker, author, life coach, and a storyteller. My work over the past 20 years has been focused in the areas of healing, initiation, grief, leadership, diversity, and inclusion.

I have a background in Organizational Management and Development with a concentration in Integral Theory which has supported me in looking at the world in a more holistic way. I also have had the privilege of studying with some amazing elders. Including Sobonfu Somé and Jojopah Maria Nsoroma, keepers of ancient indigenous wisdom from the Dagara Tribe of Burkina Faso, and Fanchon Shur in Embodying Creative Leadership through Growth in Motion. I hope my work honors them.

AMY HOWTON

I am a healer, facilitator, and weaver of stories. I listen to the stories that want to be shared and included in the weaving of new stories, ever more wonderful and true. My work over the past twenty years has focused in the areas of trauma response, racial + gender justice, leadership and evaluation, community building, social change + communal healing, and spiritual formation.

The natural world has been my most enduring classroom, grounding my practice in living systems, systems thinking, and emergent theory. I have taught at the university-level and practiced in various contexts including higher education, community-based nonprofits, faith-based institutions with experience working with individuals, organizations, and in network-building. I hold an MA in Women's, Gender, and Sexuality Studies and a doctorate in Ecological Counseling. I am a licensed professional counselor in the state of Ohio, experienced in participatory action research and human-centered design and trained in the Art of Hosting. I am the visionary and midwife of Wild Roots, Inc.; for more information visit www.wildrootsinc.com. I've had the privilege of studying and training with wise elders and guides including Margaret Wheatley, Jerry Granelli, John Milton, Quanita Roberson, and Tenneson Woolf.

Kentucky is my home, where I am surrounded by my hubby, my plants, my beasts (including our three children!), and my books. I sing and dance every chance I get and revel in the delight of mortifying my kiddos when I do. I believe laughter is the best medicine and crack myself up all the time...because what's the fun in taking ourselves so seriously?

MANY THANKS
To our community contributors.

This book was a communal effort. Over the past fifteen years that this book has been in the making, people have shown up to offer their gifts in contribution. We are both so grateful for their ability to listen to what was theirs to do and for their generosity in offering it to us.

Toby Christensen
Jojopahmaria Nsoroma
Tenneson Woolf
Timi Singley
Daven Roberson
Rita Stull
Christina Baldwin
Katie Boone
Debra Eberhardy
Rashida Manuel
David Eyman
Rick Warm
Alisdair Smith
Mama Pat
Mama Liz
Fanchon Shur
Rita Fierro
Nilima Bhat
Krister Linder
Joe Meirose
Beth Murphy
Robert Murphy
Sobonfu Somé
Malidoma Patrice Somé
Mary + St. Simon's Episcopal Church

www.ingramcontent.com/pod-product-compliance
Lightning Source LLC
Chambersburg PA
CBHW051156290426
44109CB00022B/2488